THE
PRECIPICE
OF
MENTAL
HEALTH

THE
PRECIPICE
OF
MENTAL
HEALTH

Becoming
Your Own
Safe Space

ACHEA REDD

The Precipice of Mental Health:
Becoming Your Own Safe Space

Published by Forefront Books.

Cover Design by Bruce Gore, Gore Studio Inc.
Interior Design by Linda Bourdeaux

ISBN: 978-1-63763-061-7 print
ISBN: 978-1-63763-062-4 e-book

Depression is an endless subject because people experience it so differently.

To Achea René Redd

(Me)

TABLE OF CONTENTS

FOREWORD

There is a war going on with mental health in this country—and it spreads beyond our borders. It is a battle of the minds. *The Precipice of Mental Health* is about the broader acknowledgment of mental health. Just as for any concern, you have to be able to acknowledge it and discuss it to work toward solutions to change it. One of the primary reasons that parents, spouses, family members, friends, and some people in general don't understand mental health is that they don't see what you see or feel what you feel. One of the reasons group counseling exists is so people can connect through similar experiences; they are not necessarily the same but it gives them the platform to express themselves and learn from others who understand them.

Still, it's disheartening that some individuals must be in that position before they can empathize or understand you. It can be difficult for those with anxiety, depression, or other forms of mental health challenges to hear people say they don't understand it because they haven't experienced it. Similarly, you don't have to be a doctor with cancer to treat cancer. Part of the solution is learning about mental health and what it can look like. Researching or asking the individual in order to learn more is the first step in showing that you care.

Mental health is a societal concern. We must work together to bring awareness and education to light rather than keep the issues hidden in the darkness where they will only fester. We have to put forth more effort listening to people before they reach that precipice of mental health. The point of *The Precipice of Mental Health* is to take a closer look at some of the ways anxiety and depression can affect you or those you love. It reveals Achea's journey and the damage it caused her along the way through a lack of acknowledgment, validation, and understanding throughout her childhood and into adulthood. This book, her journey, will help you realize that we have a long way to go to comprehend and accept rather than judging people who are struggling to find their balance before reaching that invisible precipice.

Achea has done a wonderful job shining a light on the darkest parts of anxiety and depression to help you understand what good mental health looks like, realize that you are not alone or stuck, and know that there are myriad resources you have available to attain it.

Alyssa Curry, LPC

ACKNOWLEDGMENTS

It was probably strange to see that I dedicated this book to myself. However, for years I have spent lots of time dumbing down the things I've accomplished and worked hard for because I was afraid to appear arrogant.

. Thankfully, through therapy I have been able to rejoice and celebrate more of my wins while dwelling less on my failures. That wouldn't have been possible without my community. First, I would like to acknowledge my "chosen family" (aka, my friends). They have been the best tribe anyone could ask for.

Thank you to Christie Angel and the entire YWCA Columbus family and Nationwide Children's Hospital Foundation's *On Our Sleeves* campaign for taking a chance on me and giving me my very first speaking engagements. Thank you for allowing me to be me and caring so much about the mental health of all those within your care.

Thank you to my entire mental health team at OSU, World of Hope Counseling, and Kovacs Counseling. You all have been and continue to be so instrumental in my recovery. Your compassion amazes me. I'm truly blessed to know you.

To my publicity team, social media team, writers, and publishers who have helped me shape my thoughts into this beautiful masterpiece, I am now and will always be grateful to all of you.

Mom, I know this book was tough to read, but you did it anyway. I love you so much.

I love you Michael, MII, and Ardyn to the moon and back. You have seen me at my worst and still love me. You make me better and inspire me to become the best version of myself.

Last, to my loyal supporters and followers. We've been through some stuff together and we have grown some too. Thank you for sticking with me, continuing to support the mission of mental health, and normalizing the conversation.

INTRODUCTION

The past rarely visits us on its own. It can bring with it situations or events that we don't want to think about or feel a connection to—we want to leave them behind. It seems that something always brought my past to the surface, as though I were reliving the trauma. The triggers that brought everything to the forefront were still in existence, and they probably still are, but what's critical is understanding that triggers that come from the past are more dangerous than you may realize. Repeatedly talking about the past isn't going to change any of that history, but it can keep me there and cause more damage by replaying the most painful or negative aspects of my life.

My mental illness serves as evidence of my past. But wasting more time or years wondering why my father was the way he was will not change him or the situation. I've acknowledged that it's not worth revisiting. When you walk away from history, use those past experiences to prevent anything like that from happening again. Determine what changes to make in your life so that you can heal. I share with you small inserts or pieces of history, such as my relationship with my father, to show you that I understand my growth and you can too.

In telling my story, I am choosing to glance into the past to learn from it rather than relive it. I've finally chosen to step out of that dark phase and into a healthier chapter of my life. This is about taking ownership of what you *can* control. Perhaps my journey will inspire you to become more self-aware so you can do renovations where they're needed.

This is my journey, and what I've gathered thus far.

CHAPTER 1

THE BEGINNING OF THE END

Over time I've learned that healing isn't linear, and recovery isn't either. Regardless of the situation, I've experienced moments of recovery and healing from depression, but just like a readout on a heart monitor, it has peaks and valleys. Situations occurred in the recovery periods that took me back to an unhealthy place during my childhood. You know—triggers. We all have them, but not all of us have healthy coping skills or know how to manage them appropriately when they're activated. During some of those devastating moments, I did my best to avoid being upset or pushed toward a setback so I wouldn't drown in depression. I learned to focus on being present rather than the beginning of my story.

For many years all the distractions of life helped me appear as though I was doing all right—until I wasn't. Truth be told, for the most part you know when you're not all right. You always know. When uncomfortable situations arose, when people joked about or said things that didn't agree with me internally, I had the propensity to blow it completely out of proportion. My dad's criticism of me became a trigger, and I developed a particularly hyper-sensitive nature. It wasn't normal and I knew it, but that's just the way I was at the time. I had the proclivity to take one thought and expand it into something bigger than intended. If I perceived someone were yelling at me, perhaps it was just their passionate tone but I some-times took it as anger. And like a hamster on a wheel, I repeatedly replayed the situation and obsessed over it, which only led me to negative self-talk because I thought I wasn't making that person happy.

I wanted to please people. In group settings and general conversation I'd rehearse conversa-tions in my head, overanalyzing what I thought I said that was stupid. Then I'd rehearse the whole moment and go over what I could have done or said differently, and when my mind took off, it ran rampant. I overanalyzed how I came across to people far more often than I should have. I was focused on controlling my tone and I tried to keep it even and upbeat to please everyone and make them feel comfortable. I often found myself doing things I didn't want to do because I felt an internal obligation to make people happy even when I wasn't happy. It was my way of trying to fit in, although I was aware that I didn't.

When you're used to depression or have accepted it as part of your life, you just want to get out of that hole and back to your "normal" as quickly as possible. Consciously and subconsciously I've stayed busy enough to circumvent the many symptoms of depression so that the impact isn't as hard. But with anxiety or depression, in time, you can become acutely aware of those moments when they start creeping up on you. The problem is that you may not know how to handle them.

I didn't want anyone going through what I'd gone through: internalizing anxiety or tightly packing in depression so it wouldn't show until I—well, *imploded*. I knew the feeling well. Anxiety and depression had traveled with me everywhere—from home to school and church—waiting for an opportunity to take over. The only time I didn't seem to have anxiety as a child at home was when I was in my bedroom. Anywhere else, that anxious feeling flooded me. My room became my cave, my closet, my

When you're used
to depression or
have accepted it
as part of your
life, you just want
to get out of that
hole and back
to "your" normal
as quickly
as possible.

safe space. If I wasn't forced to sit at the table, I preferred to eat in my bedroom and do homework there. When I was old enough to work, I didn't have as much anxiety because I didn't have any standard to meet other than the basic work criteria. I didn't have problems with customers because they didn't know me.

When it comes to life, we're not suddenly dropped into the middle of a situation to falter and figure our way out. None of us is. When we're prepared to have an honest reflection, we can pinpoint the onset of that problem or uncomfortable situation. I say "honest reflection" because we can always see what we want to see. Nevertheless, there are multiple perspectives— and then there is the truth, which is critical to our mental and physical health.

On occasion, our truth and *the truth* are two different things. Our experiences shape our truth and narrative. Over time, that has been a constant area of growth for me because my truth hasn't always been fact. When you are diagnosed with anxiety and depression, the illness may create or contribute to your analysis of *the truth*. Truth and facts can be different, and they need to be separated to find *the truth*. Overthinking can cause anxiety. Depression is a liar, and I've found it can be the same with anxiety. But there is some truth in my truth. Although my triggers weren't always based on facts, they were derived from facts. If you want to get to the root of reality, identify what facts support your truth. When I have anxiety, I have difficulty doing just that, and this is when I know that, somehow, I need to stop the anxiety. It's good to have healthy reinforcements.

See, there's a beginning to everything— which is often forgotten when problems ensue. But if you pause long enough to think back to when you fell in love, a relationship ended, you changed for better *or* worse, someone became sick, or anything traumatic happened—whatever prompted that occurrence is *the beginning*. That's the point in time when something is set into motion.

At times you may not want to remember particular periods in your life because they're too painful, so perhaps you suppress them or don't talk about them. Then, some people in your life may not want you to recall specific points that caused you harm or pain because it could be incriminating to them, but *you will*, even if it's when you're desperately trying to figure out your life so you can fix it. If you get the answers you're trying to dig up (for closure), those answers can open up more pain. What you choose to do with those memories or that history will not only shape your life, but your emotional well-being as well.

Looking back, I realized that I first began suffering from anxiety and depression in middle school. I could feel something was wrong. Of course, I didn't know what it was but I felt lumps in my throat as if someone had their hands around my neck, constricting my ability to swallow. My mouth became watery as if I were about to vomit. I'd have cold sweats and then a torrent of tears followed. I thought this happened because my feelings were hurt. I was told I had to toughen up. I needed to hear those words, but I also needed to address my internal imbalance before I could work on cultivating resiliency. I couldn't comprehend what was taking place because I experienced low moods, fatigue, loss of interest in activities, appetite changes, panic attacks, sleep difficulties, and other emotional problems as a result of what I'd gone through. I felt that everything I was taking in was suffocating me. Situations that trigger anxiety and depression affect everyone differently. It's important to understand how and where that impact comes.

It seemed as though depression hit me all at once, when in reality, slowly yet consistently, it had been coursing its way through my veins, or should I say, my brain, all along. It may not have been noticeable to others because I tried to manage by hiding it. How? By *acting* normal. I hid what was going on inside me by hiding behind an exterior facade.

When I was in middle and high school, I took care of my hair and always dressed, well, like a girly tomboy with baggy pants and fitted tops. When I smiled or laughed, I could light up any room. But none of that changed the way I felt internally. I'd shine brightly on the outside, but that light didn't make it inside—it wouldn't come on if I needed it internally, and I couldn't change that. Still, I enjoyed being at a friend's house, laughing and being silly. If I was home, usually I was in my bedroom watching *Family Matters*, *Growing Pains*, *Who's the Boss?*, *The Fresh Prince of Bel-Air*, and *A Different World*. I took little bits and pieces of the characters' television lives and tried to imagine them in mine. Looking at their lives made me believe normalcy was because the parents didn't fight all the time. *A Different World* gave me something to aspire to—going away to college, having a boyfriend, and living the life I choose. Naturally I had moments of normalcy and wonderful times with my family, but they were short-lived because my mental illness had already been set in motion.

Laughter wasn't a regular or natural occurrence in our home unless Dad was happy—so I learned to suppress joyful emotions, which became a core part of my personality. I was emotionally mature and more serious than most, which didn't help me fit into most friendships or relationships. Whenever I felt energy that wasn't good, I refrained from being physically affectionate and became quiet. That may have given the appearance that I was conceited, which impacted social connections. I sensed that allowing anyone who wasn't necessarily healthy to have too much influence over me gave them authority to shape my life and emotional well-being. You might not notice this happening at the time, but it will eventually unfold and become clear to you. That's what happened to me.

Time and experience have helped me learn to pay attention to how I feel mentally and physically when I am around others. It took me a while, but I've learned not to be dismissive of *my* feelings. Sometimes patterns can be an indication of something that needs to change. I don't allow anyone to make me think it's just me, as though I'm overanalyzing any situation. I discovered the hard way that when I'm uncomfortable, it's time to change or leave that environment. There is nothing wrong with leaving a situation instead of waiting for it to trigger you. You're the one who will deal with the ramifications if you don't remove yourself from that situation. I couldn't do that when I was a child, but now I know that when you're dismissive of what you feel, you're teaching yourself *not* to trust yourself. It's best to address these issues early on rather than allow them to go unchecked and disrupt your life when you least expect it.

Addressing what I felt helped me find my voice and empowered me in the process. I came to understand that it weeds out honest people from those who aren't. When people are honest, they can handle open, straightforward dialogue. I wasn't soliciting arguments or debates, but I needed to know who was in my corner. I didn't want to reside in a space where I was misunderstood or hadn't given people an opportunity to understand me, so I sought clarity.

Most of us were children when what we are dealing with now happened or began. However, when you are old enough to know better, do your best not to hesitate when it comes to taking care of yourself. I showed hesitation because I ignored the intuition that I'd felt at a young age. I believe we all have that discernment and intuition, and I had to learn that what was good for others wasn't necessarily suitable for me.

***

I had
to learn
that what
was good
for others
wasn't
necessarily
suitable
for me.

Four years ago I started blogging about anxiety disorders and struggles with my body. I wanted to help others while also trying to help make sense of my own history. I was always transparent about my mental health experiences and what I wanted others to learn from them, but I wasn't quite as transparent about the fact that I was still going through those issues. In part, I was so busy doing what I love, which is helping others, that I wasn't feeling my mental health issues ripping me apart as much as they were.

People carry pain and trauma as though it's normal, but no—it's not. And at some point you will be forced to let it go or accept account-ability for allowing it to become an unbear-able weight that kills your spirit or *you*. When that happens you can become emotionally numb, despondent, or dissociated, which are all unhealthy coping mechanisms. Pretending to be engaged in conversation, having difficulty connecting to your environment, and feeling as though you're the outsider in your own life can wear on you. And those are warnings. If they

persist, depression can become so dark that it
buries you.

Every day, countless people are *just* going
through the motions—spouses, children, rela-
tives, friends, colleagues, business partners, or
someone who hands you a cup of coffee at the
local bakery. You may not know it because they
still smile and may appear to be quite normal,
but don't underestimate the power of depression.
Whether you're struggling with anxiety, depression, body dysmorphia, addiction, or something
else, it had a beginning. When people choose
to die by suicide, that choice had a beginning,
too, and something led them to take that path
rather than another. If we want to get to the
root of our problems, we need to see them for
what they are, not what we want them to be,
and the same goes for how we see people and
even ourselves. The optics matter. Have honest
conversations. Learn how to reconcile problems, adverse history, and hurtful emotions.
We can't change history. Nevertheless, we can
change ourselves.

For many years, when I thought about my
life, I wanted the memories to change and be

....

We can't change history. Nevertheless, we can change ourselves.

....

something other than what they were. Perhaps I wanted the life or family that people thought we had. I kept trying to figure out why things hurt or affected me so I could at least try to have a chance at a healthier life. But instead, I kept going back and bringing the dysfunction and pain to the forefront. In doing so, I gave it relevance. If you know what I'm expressing, it's because you've given the past power over your life too. The sad thing about it is that most often the people who hurt you the most don't realize it, they don't care, or perhaps they've asked for forgiveness and moved on. No matter what the reason is, we have to do the same. We need to learn how to release unnecessary baggage and forgive ourselves in the process.

When dysfunctional or hurtful situations occur, we think forgiveness lets someone off the hook, but it's not about that. That's not the intent of forgiveness either. Forgiveness is about freeing yourself from the negative emotions you've been left with because they prevent you from moving forward in a healthier way. More importantly, forgiveness helps us have a better relationship with ourselves, and we are kinder because that anger or hate is no longer present. Our conversations aren't filled with negative dialogue of what was or what should have been. Forgiveness is a part of a healthy process that creates a healthier mindset. Besides, if things keep triggering you, it's important to learn how to let go of unnecessary emotional baggage. Counseling provided me a space to untangle negative emotions, process unhealthy thoughts, and begin to decrease triggers.

I grew up in a household where Mom taught me to be a strong black woman like her mom had been. And Dad raised me to be tough like a guy; he didn't want me to let my emotions show. He wanted me to be masculine toward other people—in relationships and with friends. He told me, "Never let anyone see you sweat, let them in, or admit anything." And he emphasized, "Go to your grave with your secrets." The crazy part was that he wanted me to be like that with everyone but him. Oh, and Dad was a pastor—so this really created an internal conflict. His advice felt hypocritical, contrary to what a pastor or man of God would align his beliefs with or teach anyone. It never settled with me, but I did as I was instructed. I didn't see the harm in trusting my father at that age.

When we're taught to hide something, we learn how to lie, not only to others but to ourselves. And at some point the boundaries of truth are moved or stretched further each time. The highest price I paid was in terms of my body. Stress isn't solely mental or emotional. It affects all systems of the body. I have migraines and digestive issues, which come from the pressure I put on myself. When I went to my neurologist, one of the first questions he asked was, "What is your life like?" because that is relevant. The ability to process and cope with stress gives one person the edge over another. It is damaging to your health to hide your truth and refrain from forgiving people. It's taken me a long time to learn that what happened in the past and forgiveness isn't necessarily about others; it's about you and your well-being. Letting go releases the pain and anger and the anxiety and depression that comes from reliving things.

Whether Dad knew it or not, he was creating a duality within me. Everyone else got the happy, outgoing, and fun version of me;

and, as he requested, he got the other version: the quiet and submissive me. I had opposing personalities, and my core beliefs weren't necessarily mine. I was told that my productivity defined who I was as a person. I was taught to be strong—but not too strong—and I often wondered what that meant.

Many other core beliefs were embedded in me that caused an internal conflict because instinctively I disagreed with them. I was trying to sustain some semblance of my real self when I wasn't around my family, but at home I was gradually becoming the child my father was shaping. It became more and more challenging to undo the beliefs and perceptions he was teaching me, and those transferred into adulthood and eventually my marriage. Because of the deception I witnessed Dad practice, and yes, considering his position in the community, I didn't trust people—especially men. I think it was because I was aware of the inconsistent and dishonest way he lived. I deemed it unfathomable to accept how easily people in the church fell for it. Naturally, people believe what they want, yet they are more inclined to trust their pastor, priest, or minister.

We were an example of what a family should look like to the outside world—happy, prosperous, spiritual, and highly favored. But behind closed doors we were not what anyone would strive to be—we were *highly dysfunctional*. One of the factors that allowed the dysfunction to continue and manifest in my adult life to the degree that it did is that I stayed home longer than I should have rather than do what I thought would have been best for me. People need to be themselves.

Before I began college, Dad told me to go into broadcasting or be a preacher; it's what he chose for me. I didn't love or have a passion for either, but I was inclined to do what I was told. The only love I had was what he told me I should have. My first semester of college I studied general education; the second semester, I took psychology and sociology. Halfway through the semester, my professor stopped me after class and asked, "What's your major?"

I told her, "Communications."

Her eyes smiled as she said, "I would consider changing it because you have something special. I see students all the time and I know a psychology brain when I see it. You could have a *bright* future."

It was the first time anyone had ever seen me for who I was and didn't give me a label or expectations of whom I was supposed to be. Instead, she gave me encouragement that aligned with what I believed. I felt so empowered because no one had ever said anything like that to me before. I went home super excited and told Dad that my psychology professor thought I should change my major to psychology. He curtly replied, "That would be the stupidest thing you would ever do in your life! Ain't nobody coming to talk to no black woman! I'm not paying for that!"

It crushed me and made me feel that what I was showing my professor wasn't real, and that Dad saw I wasn't bright enough to do well in psychology. Though this derailed an opportunity to discover who Achea was, it didn't have to be final. Ultimately, we can get back to where we were always meant to be.

★★★

It was supposed to be my first semester as a freshman at Ohio Dominican. I was accepted to this college out of state, and I was excited about beginning my journey. As the time came for me to leave, I spent a week boxing up books, trinkets, clothing, shoes, and things that would make me feel like I was in my safe haven—my bedroom. When I looked at Mom, she was sad. Not only could I see it, I felt it. She wouldn't cross the threshold into my bedroom to help me get my things ready for the big transition to my new college, and that wasn't like her. Ultimately, I made the decision not to go away to school because I couldn't leave Mom. That didn't feel right. Although I wasn't able to reverse or undo anything, I had become her confidant. I felt she needed me, and perhaps I needed her, too, in a codependent way. I chose to stay at home, so I can't make any excuses. But I will say that sometimes it's hard to leave the only thing you know. Most of the damage had been done, but it continued longer than necessary. The results were sure to show at some point.

I achieved my degree while working at my father's church in the ministry resources center handling the audiotapes of his sermons while managing the store and making sure his messages were duplicated. Even there, I faced an inner struggle from the fact that I was perpetuating the same behaviors as my father: living one way while teaching people that they should be living a different way. That internal conflict eventually resolved, and I never got into drugs or alcohol, but I did have a dysfunction interlaced with food and losing myself.

I'm certain my parents hoped their dysfunctional behaviors would stay within their relationship and inside the walls of our house, but those memories have caused tremendous turmoil and displaced emotions in me. I absorbed the dysfunction as it was allocated; it was in the air at home and in church. It tightly coiled inside me and when it emerged it was in the form of painful stomachaches, an eating disorder, and body dysmorphia when I was twelve. The stress manifested as irritable bowel syndrome (IBS) by high school, and at nineteen, I went to the hospital because of chronic pain. A test revealed my bowels were impacted up to my ribcage. They asked Mom what was going on in my life that caused me to be so stressed at such a young age. The doctor went on to tell Mom he thought I had depression.

Mom never verbally acknowledged that my home life was responsible for these symptoms, so it was unaddressed for many years. I've had digestive issues since I was three and have been given laxatives and enemas to try to correct the problems. The migraines became more frequent and all I could do was suffer in darkness. Everything happening to me physically, mentally, and emotionally was in some way connected to what happened in our house. And when I was old enough to understand this, it was the beginning of the end. My life began unraveling and spiraling, though I fought to hold it together as long as possible. I thought I did OK struggling in silence. I managed by putting Band-Aids over everything that hurt so I didn't embarrass my family.

It wasn't until I left home, married my husband, Michael, in 2006, and had children that I recognized my remedies for holding myself together weren't working. To avoid embarrassing my family, I went to church, had pastoral counseling, prayed, and exercised seemingly to no avail. Unable to continue treating myself, I finally sought therapy in my thirties. I had to find a solution or some sense of balance because I didn't love myself—*at all*. Detached and critical of myself, I didn't have time to discover my identity, so I kept building on the false one I was living.

One day I woke up and wondered who the hell I was—I surely didn't know. I wanted to take better care of myself, to be whole for my husband and children, so I had to figure it out. I tried, but apparently what I was doing wasn't enough. And as much as Michael loves me, and as strong as he is, even he was rendered powerless when I was diagnosed with anxiety and depression. Although he was empathetic to what I was going through, he didn't fully understand the scope of what I was dealing with. Sometimes something more powerful than you will cause

I didn't have
time to discover
my identity, so I
kept building on
the false one I
was living.

you to face reality, whether you're ready or not—and it was my time.

Recognizing the origin of your issues and triggers doesn't necessarily mean you have to dive deep into the past, but you can identify critical points in your life that have influenced you. When you can acknowledge those, you are working to have more insight that can help you turn those triggers off.

What was your beginning?

CHAPTER 2

THE REALITY OF COVID-19

The first week of March in 2020, my husband, Michael, and I returned from our annual trip to Cabo San Lucas, Mexico, right before COVID-19 was announced as a pandemic. No one knew this virus would hit as hard as it did, but it brought me to complete devastation when I was already doing everything possible to hold myself together. Before we left, I spoke with my family physician given that I'd been diagnosed with generalized anxiety disorder (GAD), major depressive disorder (MDD), and body dysmorphia (BDD), and the antidepressant I was on wasn't working. I knew my body was struggling to adjust, and the last thing I wanted to do was to have depression hanging over me in Mexico while our toes were sinking into the warm sand. We were supposed to be enjoying the atmosphere—but I could feel the heaviness, and it was getting dark.

Before we left, my family doctor recommended I see a psychiatrist. Full disclosure: I was afraid to see a psychiatrist because of the stigma of doing so. Yet based on what I was feeling, I knew that I'd take his advice when I returned from Cabo. For now, I was OK with the diagnosis of clinical depression. I'd grown tired of concealing my depression to make others comfortable, but I did the best I could, and Michael sensed it. I don't think there was anything he could say. He always just seemed to know when things were a bit rough for me, and he probably thought it was something I had to work through on my own.

Even without a struggle with depression, nothing is perfect, but when I look behind me, Michael is there. I'm grateful that I'm able to feel love and admiration for my husband, especially since depression has taken a lot from me. It affects how I think, feel, and manage daily activities—basically every aspect of my life, which Michael has seen. One of the hardest things is that it took time to disconnect Michael from the stereotype of my father—and how I'd come to view men. I thought that as a woman I wasn't as good as a man because of what I witnessed and the things I heard as a child, so I felt inferior and powerless to men. Consequently, I was predisposed to never being on a level playing field when I came up against a man. After observing Dad's pathology for most of my life, I believed a man was always going to do what he was going to do. Mom allowed Dad's pathology so I never had a reason to trust men, and I didn't learn that they respected women either.

While my father was the litmus test, Michael helped me realize all men aren't the same—all people aren't the same. Michael's the best man I know, and it's disheartening that he's taken the brunt of outcomes he didn't create. Typically the person or people closest to you do. Because of him I know, beyond a shadow of a doubt, that unconditional love exists, but it doesn't cure depression. Most people experience unconditional love with someone, but depression can mute those feelings in those dark moments. Depression can remove the ability to see and feel love, support, compassion, or anything. It's essential to do your best to see your marriage or relationship for what it is, rather than what it feels like when you are battling depressive episodes—because there is a difference. *Ask the person who loves you for a reminder of what is real versus what's real in the moment.*

My marriage hits an emotional place in me, and it always has because I love my husband.

It's essential to do your best to see your marriage or relationship for what it is, rather than what it feels like when you are battling depressive episodes— because there is a difference.

Regardless of what I've gone through, that hasn't changed. Is our marriage perfect all the time? No. But what is? I see who Michael is as an individual, husband, father, and athlete, and he's consistent—it's the situations that change. When conditions change, sometimes people do. And if you have depression, know that it's a highly recurrent disorder so your responses to problems may differ. The difficult part is that I didn't want to disappoint my husband, but with anxiety and depression, he's on that ride with me. When someone gets in the car that you're driving and you crash, they crash too. The damage to them may not be as severe, but the experience is real. When you are diagnosed with depression, anxiety, an eating disorder, or something else, you know what you have. You may be seeing a therapist, psychiatrist, or taking medications needed to help you find balance, but who supports your spouse, children, friends, and others around you when they feel hopeless? In many ways, depression affects the whole team. If you're down, the team is dysfunctional.

Mom was at a loss, my husband was confused, and my children didn't know how to process what I was going through because, well, they were children. On the other hand, my husband kept things organized and moving. As my husband came to understand my illness, he became careful with me emotionally. I was dealing with several situations based on historical insight in a way that I'd never been subjected to before. I was volatile because of the unhealed trauma that came in consonance with it.

My son wanted to fix me, like his dad, while my daughter treated me the same as always. She knew I'd changed but didn't treat me any differently. When my husband and son appeared unaffected and unbothered, it hurt me. I was afraid. I wanted my husband to stop and notice that I wasn't OK, and perhaps he did, but it would have been in his nature to handle the situation as he deemed best. Michael had the proficiency to compartmentalize issues and continue as usual since there was nothing he could do. He kept the house floating along healthily by sustaining a sense of normalcy for our children; they still needed their parents.

While we may feel that people don't care or that someone's indifferent to what we're going through, that mentality is unhealthy and can be further damaging. People who love us and have been supportive aren't out to get us or hurt us; it's more than likely that they don't know how to respond. Unless they've been trained on how to handle someone with depression, that's normal. During that period and in those moments I was self-centered in my thinking, and I couldn't see things from anyone's lens but my own.

How do you see it?

Depression and anxiety can cause a limited view because your thoughts are about how things impact *you* rather than those around you. You're too busy fighting the riptide, suffocating, failing, or plunging to your demise, and can't seem to make it back up to the edge of reality. When that's happening, everything—and I mean *everything*—is about surviving.

As it relates to depression or anxiety, admittedly, there were occasions when I was self-centered and my life was about me because

I desperately needed help. I clearly didn't know the right way to convey that to anyone. But there had to come a time in my recovery when I turned the corner. I still had to be accountable for my actions and change the narrative, even in moments of weakness and anxiety when I wasn't as strong and didn't feel like myself.

For quite some time, I remained hesitant to share my fears and the details of my struggles with Michael. I couldn't handle suppressing my emotions well, so I cried a lot but disguised it to lessen the worry and shame of being unable to manage them. I'd tell Michael and my children I was praying. That's what that duality taught me. But again, if no one knew the depths of my depression and the pain it caused, how could they help me?

Michael's personality is strong. He doesn't focus on things such as fears and struggles, and that's because he's not just an athlete—he's a true competitor. He's the crème de la crème. Michael won a gold medal in the 2008 Olympics and played twelve years in the NBA. He has the drive, discipline, and resilience to accomplish *anything* he desires. Once Michael retired, he

reinvented himself and kept going. I admire that
and wish I could be that way and see things
the way he does. But it doesn't make it easy to
talk to him. He's dismissive of history because
he wants to look *forward*. I didn't know how to
garner the strength or ability to do that. I asked
Michael how that works, and he said, "I don't
know how it works. You just do it." But the
truth is, it's innate for him. That's the epitome of
how he was raised, and that's *his* beginning. I'm
very practical, and in certain situations I need
someone to tell me what to do and how to do it.
I needed the guidance to overcome some of the
adversities I've faced, but my depression doesn't
make me easy to help.

Like you or perhaps others, I have a history
that wasn't always the best. The problem is that I
was choosing to stay connected to the individual
who negatively affected me the most, and therefore I was staying connected to all the things
that triggered my anxiety and depression. I
thought it would help me determine *why* things
happened the way they did. All the while, I kept
myself on the line, constantly ruminating over
something I'd never know the answer to. If I let

**If I let it go,
I felt I was
letting my father
off the hook.**

it go, I felt I was letting my father off the hook. That's the reason I hadn't forgiven him. I wanted Dad to be held accountable for the damage he caused me. I wanted him to say something that it took me years to recognize he wasn't capable of: "I'm sorry." You have to humble yourself and put yourself in the other person's shoes to see the ways you've hurt them, but he wasn't willing to do that. My father taught me not to disclose personal or family business and take my secrets to the grave—why didn't I expect him to do the same? He seemed to create chaos and slide right past everything flawlessly. He was a pastor, and that was his "free pass."

I tried not to let Michael detect my concern about seeing a psychiatrist, but I was on the cusp of something I was afraid of because it was bigger than me, and I needed help. When I spoke to him about it, I tried to be upbeat and positive rather than express my fears. Cabo is my happy place, so I tried hard not to focus on anything other than my husband while we were there. I was with him. *I was happy*. But at one point when I was alone getting a massage, I started thinking about the worst-case scenario.

Since I didn't know what was wrong and why I'd gotten so bad, I was afraid the psychiatrist would diagnose me with something more severe. Knowing that Michael saw things from a positive perspective, taking a negative approach to this would only annoy him; I decided not to bring it up so we could enjoy our vacation. Sometimes we want others to be OK because depression belongs to us. It can cause feelings of emptiness, irritability, low energy, loss of interest, difficulty sleeping, and fatigue, but I guess I had gotten used to it.

It didn't help that we returned to Ohio's typical weather pattern in March—overcast, cold, and raining—when I craved the warmth of the sun and fresh air. They helped me with the chemical imbalance, but without it, that magnetic pull toward the precipice was stronger. Things I hadn't been properly addressing had become more prominent, and the impact was immediate.

As recommended by my family doctor, I met with a psychiatrist. He was a calm, gentle soul who spoke to me like a therapist. He was not only going to help get my medicine right, he did therapy too. He was weaning me off one medication and putting me on another. The process was problematic. I started having withdrawal symptoms, and it took eight to ten weeks to adjust to the new prescription. I have beautiful children and a husband who loves me, yet I didn't want to get up, shower, or eat. I started getting flulike symptoms and having terrible brain zaps. When I explained what I was feeling, he increased my new medication; then I had insomnia. I wasn't happy and I wasn't sad—I was just numb. It felt as though my brain was being toyed with and I couldn't do anything about it.

For some families, moms are like the thermostat in the house; they make it a home and create warmth. But *I* wasn't working because the climate in our home was becoming emotionally cold. Adding to that stress, COVID-19 became a pandemic. Like much of the country, we took the CDC's precautions—playing it safe, masking, and limiting social interactions. I didn't know it then, but that was going to be problematic for me.

Before the coronavirus hit, I was on a fast trajectory of speaking and being out in public sharing my first book, *Be Free. Be You.* That gave me something I needed, and I looked forward to validation from others. Once COVID-19 hit I was home with my husband and two precious children, Ardyn, ten, and Michael, thirteen. I wasn't out there speaking, working, or interacting with friends as much. I didn't have those distractions. I was home where I'd walk past a mirror barely recognizing myself. My reflection told me I wasn't happy. I tried to justify it by placing blame on the fact that I wasn't busy.

When I spoke to my psychiatrist, I addressed concern over how I felt—the emptiness—and he said, "You need to feel worthy whether you are speaking to one person or a thousand people. You don't think you have an internal worth. You have it—it's suppressed, but you have to expose it."

That caused me to pause and wonder if there was something to what he was saying. I've been in therapy sessions where my therapist has probably said those same words to me, but I wasn't ready to receive them. When someone tells you that you don't have an internal worth, that's not what you want to hear. Who does?

You don't think you have an internal worth. You have it— it's suppressed, but you have to expose it.

We all want or need to feel we have value to someone, especially ourselves. Those words caused me to stand at the mirror a bit longer, looking for it. They caused me to say, "What is it about Achea that you *like* and *love*?" I should have thought about the things I do well or how I care about people and love people, but my response was, "Nothing." I walked away thinking, *Wow! I don't have one single thing I like or love about myself.*

For about eight weeks, I held everything inside. I think COVID-19 added to the pressure. Again, before COVID-19 hit, I was on a roll. When people told me I was great—I *was* great. Those positive affirmations felt good. I was out speaking, promoting my book, visiting with friends, and making a difference by helping others, but when the pandemic hit, all that was shut down. I thought the love that people had for me was performance-based.

When people said, "God is your Father," I realized that I didn't have a good relationship with Dad. My father never made me feel worthy or happy, and I didn't trust a relationship with the God he taught us to worship. My goodness had always been based on what I did, not who I was. And now I really couldn't do anything! The reality of my life was closing in on me, and it felt suffocating.

I was already having a rough time. I'd gained a little weight and wasn't able to exercise the way I typically would. I didn't have the outward physical appearance I had always worked to keep up. If one of your parents has taught you to hold everything in and not let anyone see the real you, all you have to work with is your exterior. I looked around and saw my beautiful family and home and I didn't understand how I could be numb but still cry when I wasn't sad. I would cry. I couldn't get out of bed. It appeared that I had adjusted to the medication in terms of my symptoms because they decreased. However, the depression increased.

How did I know it was bad? Well, not only was I thinking of not getting up, I was thinking about divorce or getting in my car and driving away from my family because I felt they deserved better. They hadn't done anything to deserve what I was feeling or thinking. They were casualties of depression. If you have depression, you have some of those too. Generally when I had these moments of depression the kids were in school. Now they were home all day due to COVID-19. Michael was home all day too. I no longer had the energy or capability to fake being OK. Crying without being seen was impossible. I couldn't control it.

In April, we were quarantined at home due to the escalating numbers of people with COVID-19. Part of my new schedule was homeschooling Ardyn and Michael. They weren't the problem; it was that it became more difficult for me to hide my depression. When they were at school, they didn't necessarily see it—not the way they could now. Sure, they knew about my diagnosis; I'm honest and upfront about that. But no one knew it had gotten to the low point it had.

I'd reached the precipice of mental health, and I'd fallen right off that cliff.

Imagine how many other people probably went off that same precipice because of COVID-19. Substance abuse, suicidal ideation, anxiety disorders, and depressive disorders increased. The stay-at-home order left some quarantined with their significant other whom they may have discovered they didn't like. There were articles and news reports about the demand for therapists, and people were doing online therapy sessions because of need. When you can come and go as you please and have an outlet through friendships, working out at a gym, socializing at work, church, or whatever—it can help anyone's mental health. But when COVID-19 got worse and the numbers escalated, those options didn't exist. Parents were responsible for their children on a full-time basis. Many had to homeschool their children, and numerous others worked from home.

When things were shut down, people didn't have their standard outlets or regular outings and gatherings with friends. Some were completely isolated. The effects that COVID-19 would have on mental health were not always considered. It seemed that nothing other than isolation kept people alive. Diminishing hope contributed to an increase in suicides and drug overdoses (according to ADAMH, NAMI, and The Suicide Prevention Hotline). Only essential workers

were going to work. As time went on, countless people lost their jobs. When unemploy-
ment benefits ran out for some, another layer
of stress was compounded on top of everything
else. Stress evolved from the state of the nation
caused by the pandemic. In the beginning, there
were no concerts, no sports—*nothing*.

The coronavirus forced everyone to take a
microscopic look at their reality and decide if
they could handle it. I suppose that's something
we should consider doing regularly. If they didn't
know, they'd find out. COVID-19 amplified
anxiety, depression, and brokenness. For some
who didn't have depression before, it developed after COVID-19 hit. Nearly everyone was
dealing with significant stress and psychological
distress, also known as *change*.

When someone asks how you're doing, they
typically expect you to say "Good" or "Great!"
even when you're not—and when they know
you're not. Sometimes they really don't want to
hear about how you're feeling or what you're
dealing with, primarily when they've heard it
before and the conversation or situation remains
the same. You don't magically get better from

depression, and sometimes your responses don't change. Besides, people have problems of their own. Your problems, illness, anxiety, depression—that gets old to them. *You and I both know it gets old to just about everyone.* But that's our life. It's another new day and struggle for those of us with anxiety, depression, or other mental health issues.

The morning my life seemed to be internally unraveling, everything *appeared* to be as expected—but it wasn't. I knew how far from OK I had strayed—my mind was in constant undulation and the side effects of the antidepressant I was on hurled everything to another level—a hellish level. Although I was not suicidal, on occasion I had intrusive thoughts. This is similar to an intruder entering your home—you don't invite them. They break in. I didn't want to hurt or kill myself. That's not what I was feeling—it was different. I just casually thought, *God, if you don't want to wake me up today, I would be OK.* I had thoughts about death so much that I was OK with dying. Life was exhausting. In reality, of course, those thoughts weren't normal.

Until that point death had always scared me and had a negative connotation. But oddly, it was my *life* that was scaring me now. The fact that I was so calm about being OK with death was disconcerting. But tucking it all away as I'd been taught to do, I went about running my routine the way I always had—looking relatively normal in the process.

I typically set my alarm to 7:00 a.m. and even on those difficult days I'd drag myself out of bed, wake the kids to start their online schooling, trudge downstairs to brew coffee, watch *Good Morning America*, the *TODAY* show, or the news, and attempt to pull together enough energy to do household chores. It became increasingly harder to force myself to move around and clean the kitchen or try to exercise. Depression was winning. When depression eroded my energy, the last thing I could do or desired to do was to work out. Until now, this had been an outlet for me when I felt overwhelmed. Desire was one of the first things to go—along with willingness, ability, and normalcy. That morning was vastly different. I didn't want to get out of bed, but

somehow, I instantly knew I felt different. Once
you experience bouts of depression and relapse,
you become familiar with the warning signs
and symptoms.

Because I'd already seen my psychiatrist, I
knew I needed to start my recovery plan as soon
as I felt the first symptom. So I started making
the recommended adjustments. I was in the
process of changing medications and was made
aware that things would get pretty rocky before
they got better. I didn't think things could get
much worse than what I was already dealing
with, but then I hit a point where I thought,
Oh, shit. I'm in trouble! Old symptoms began
to reemerge with intensity and I was unable to
keep up the facade of being able to manage; but
in that situation, I was completely cognizant that
there was nothing I could do.

In Act One I sat in the audience watching
my life play out on stage. I was feeling more
disconnected from my family as my emotions
went numb. I was still functioning day to day,
but going through the motions was a challenge
for me. Act Two went a lot further than where
I thought it would; I didn't recognize myself.

By Act Three, I'd never looked so vividly out of control in my life. Terror blanketed my face as I watched my life flash before me—I was no longer a willing participant. This season taught me about having all the faculties of my mind. Anxiety is harsh, but depression? *It's bad and the further you fall, it's downright horrifying.*

It's strange how I had morbid thoughts, no longer wanting to be alive, and felt as though I were in the darkest frame of mind. But oddly enough, after I put on a pair of Lululemon leggings, a sweatshirt, and a smile, no one knew the difference. Don't let anyone make you think people who have mental health issues have a particular look—that's not necessarily true. I looked just fine.

When my husband got out of bed that same morning, it was impossible for him to know that I was *consumed* by darkness; I couldn't feel or see anything. The ground beneath me became unstable and suddenly collapsed. The surge of darkness rising within was terrifying because I'd been falling for some time. The weight I carried throughout most of my life finally forced my descent at a speed that caused me to lose complete control. There was nothing or no one to grab hold of to break my fall. I'd been going through the motions—desperately searching for ways to unload enough baggage and pain so I could continue existing without falling so fast. Who was I kidding? The fall was inevitable.

My smile and laughter weren't genuine. Other than pain, there was nothing left inside me. No soul. No trust. No faith. No God. No more of this. I'd grown tired of hiding my truths and my feelings about reality and questioning everything as though I was somehow wrong. It was *my* reality because it didn't belong to anyone else. No one saw the toxic turmoil ravaging my mind or the emptiness in my heart that had spilled over from my childhood—and not being understood amplified the pain. I was isolated with those feelings. I couldn't help but remember the powerful prayers, laughter, and good times that had been overshadowed by my parents' fights, Dad's adultery, demeaning adjectives, the agony it caused, unyielding silent tears, incredible mistrust, and being uncomfortable in our home. Since we didn't talk about anything that had happened and I didn't see any healthy resolutions, I practiced what I was taught, which was to internalize everything and outwardly *act* normal. To quickly prevent or diffuse unpleasant situations, I turned inward, blamed myself for everything, and pretended everyone around me was a good person and that I needed to be good too. I had high-functioning anxiety and depression. That denotes that everything I did was under the constant threat or weight of anxiety and depression, but I did my best to look normal. It's ironic because I was high functioning . . . until I wasn't.

I did such a good job pretending to be OK that when people heard me talking about what was wrong with me they were detached from emotionally caring or showing concern because it was a part of me. They were used to it, although I wasn't. Mom never asked about my eating disorder. Starving myself interrupted my growth pattern, and that, too, was never questioned. Most days, I survived on a little snack pack of Pizza Combos and a can of Dr Pepper. From twelve years old straight into those difficult high school years, I ate most of my meals in my room, and no one asked me about this or even seemed to notice. No one was curious about how or why I was losing weight or the reason I always had money (I didn't use it for lunch), and that went unnoticed too. There came a time I was so used to putting on a mask and slipping past everyone that I *became* that person with the mask. I was well cared for in a material sense, but emotionally and physically, I wasn't seen or heard. That act slowly suffocated my soul and pushed me toward a slow, agonizing emotional death.

Since Dad was a pastor, people looked to us as an example of what a family should look like, but behind closed doors, we were not what a family would want to be. It was hard to leave the only thing you know, and that's where the damage came into play. When you are used to dysfunction, a survival tactic is to adjust so you can function in it.

As with many others, COVID-19 left me with too much time on my hands, forcing me to face the reality of my life along with everything I was hiding, suppressing, or trying to escape.

CHAPTER 3

AN END TO A WELL-KEPT FACADE

Before the pandemic, people saw me at speaking events with my husband or children, dining out, or hanging with my friends, and that gave me a reason to keep myself together—externally. But during the quarantine for COVID-19, I was home with no reason to manage the facade any longer. And honestly, I didn't want to continue this way, with a false outward identity. Majorly depressed, I found it difficult and sometimes near impossible to pull myself up, get out of bed, and take a shower. There was a constant force pulling me back to bed, and with what little energy I could gather, I'd tug away just to make it to the shower where I'd get in—only to cry. My tears blended with the streams of water, washing away visible evidence of my pain.

I felt everything I'd internalized coming to a head, an unraveling of sorts, and I couldn't stop it. As soon as my feet hit the shower floor, I started sobbing harder than ever before. Although I didn't want to, I began ruminating on my past. Again. Why? Because it was there. It was always there. I wanted to feel the joy of my present, but regardless of how hard I tried,

I couldn't. My children were downstairs doing their schoolwork, and I couldn't effectively participate or help them if they needed me. The veil that hid everything had fallen, and I felt completely exposed and afraid.

I didn't want to live like this anymore. The sad thing is that at this point Michael knew I was hurting and depressed. During the process of changing medicines, I had to tell Michael why it was necessary and explain what I was experiencing. He was concerned about me, and I believed he had the right to know. Besides, the process was complex. I had to be open and honest with him so he understood what he would potentially see me go through.

It was bad. Throughout the day I cried what seemed to be nonstop over just about every-thing. It didn't matter how relevant it was; I just cried. I'd make my way to my sofa only to sit and stare out the big picture window in my living room, weeping without having a clue as to why. I wondered how I had any tears left. I couldn't sleep or concentrate, and I could hardly finish thoughts and sentences. Those were the mental changes. I became exceedingly

withdrawn and didn't engage in conversation
or laugh much. Strangely, I wasn't sad or angry.
I didn't do anything other than cry. Physically,
the process of changing medicines caused me to
have brain zaps, flulike symptoms, chills, nausea,
and a decreased appetite. My mom, who's an
excellent cook, came to cook for us, but, oddly,
nothing tasted good. Of course not everyone
with depression has the same response. Or even
if they do, the onslaught of symptoms may not
happen in the same order, but it can be harmful
in other ways. Most people think depression is
just a feeling of severe (or extreme) sadness, but
for me it produced a feeling of complete emptiness while removing my ability to feel. I suffered
in silence.

My emotional regulation is different from
that of the average individual. It's confusing to
cry while experiencing a void of emotions. We
take for granted that people should be able to
identify the reasons for their feelings—maybe
their trust was broken, someone hurt them, or
they received poor feedback at work. When
people know a reason why, it's easier to identify a solution. But I had an inability to explain

why I was sad. For people who experience a void of feelings while crying or angry, it's harder to figure out solutions on your own when you don't know the *why* of it all.

Through all the uncertainty, Michael didn't turn away or ignore me. He continued to be a strong pillar for the children and me. I have strong emotions but Michael is emotionally even. By nature, he's at a five on an emotional scale of ten while I'm at a ten *without* medicine or any depression. It wasn't always that way, but because it was *my* thing, he had to learn how to make adjustments. In any relationship there are adjustments, but certain mental health issues can be challenging, and I don't imagine that being easy for anyone.

Although I was the one dealing with depression and I was the one going through those emotions, it still impacted the rest of my family. For some, the ramifications can be destructive. The people closest to you or those you interact with regularly feel the impact of your mental health challenges, and the complexity and severity can vary. If they don't at least have an accurate understanding of it, it can

We take for granted that people should be able to identify the reasons for their feelings . . . When people know a reason why, it's easier to identify a solution.

make it worse. Thankfully, even when I couldn't grasp exactly where I was on the scale, Michael understood me. And I think he became used to the highs and lows, ups and downs, extreme sadness, and irritability. Being an athlete, he was used to adversity at the highest level, and my husband presented himself as though he could handle anything. Somehow that was tough for me because he was OK and I wasn't. That made me feel even more alone. But the reality was that he *had* to be OK to take care of our children and other responsibilities.

Given everything I was going through, Michael was right there with me. He hadn't realized how bad it really was because I'd shoved so much pain, confusion, and sadness so profoundly inside me for so many years— starting long before I'd met him. Finally, there was nowhere to put anything else, and with the force of a volcano triggered by pressure, every- thing started boiling its way out. At this point I was sure my children knew Mommy wasn't OK, and the thought of them being affected by it, too, was devastating. There are no words.

When the coronavirus pandemic worsened, I didn't have the energy to help our kids with homeschooling. But I pushed myself and felt the weight on my shoulders as I moved around. It was unbearable. What do you think their mother looked like to them? What did they have to handle? People say you should push yourself or force yourself to do something you need to do, and sure—that works with a strong and capable mind. But I had pushed myself right up to that precipice.

After sobbing through my shower and dressing with great difficulty, I dragged myself downstairs. Ardyn and Michael were at the kitchen table doing their virtual school, and my husband was occupied on a conference call in his office. After making sure they were OK with their schoolwork, I struggled to lift one leg after the other to climb the stairs to return to our bedroom. Moving was tough—there was *nothing* left in me, and at that point, I was running on fumes.

Everything I'd suppressed for years seemed as though it were erupting internally, bringing an end to a well-kept facade, and I couldn't stop

....

I had
pushed myself
right up to that
precipice.

....

it from happening. I didn't want to hide my
truth or pain. I wanted to be free of what hurt
me. My parents' lives shouldn't have become
my burden, and they shouldn't have become a
burden to my husband or children either. I'd
brought this into our lives, and I needed to
remove the damage it was doing. I watched
my father living a hypocritical life as he taught
and preached the powerful word of God to
his congregation—but his words and messages
weren't consistent.

I felt this Christianity stuff wasn't working
and I had a significant shift in my faith. It wasn't
that I hadn't tried—it was that I had. But what
I was taught versus what I saw made me question God. I thought that if *this* was what being a
Christian was all about, I didn't want any part of
it. But without God, without *that* relationship—I
felt worse. The internal conflict became so
intense that it made the depression even darker.
When COVID-19 hit, the virus hadn't touched
me but its ramifications knocked the wind out
of me. I felt locked inside my internal prison—
facing an ugly reality alone. I'd been crying on

my closet floor for three agonizing months, close to completely turning my back on God.

I was affecting my children and I knew they were confused. My anxiety shows up as irritability and snapping, and now I was crying all the time. My daughter was nine, dumbfounded and concerned about her mother. Michael was twelve and he was annoyed. He'd say, "You're crying again?" I was upset with myself because I couldn't tell them why. How do you say to your children that you don't know why you're crying and that *you* can't feel anything, when they're young and going through it with you? Since I couldn't feel anything, what if they questioned whether I felt anything for them? They hadn't done anything. The immediate thought that came to my mind was, *I'm no good for them.* The last thing I wanted to do was make them feel how I felt. I didn't want to burden my children or damage them. Growing up, I'd had to be the strong shoulder and emotional support for my own mom, and I didn't want them to become that for me. I wanted to escape and run because I thought that my family would be better off without me than with me. The overwhelming darkness and hopelessness caused me to think this was the end, and I was going to die.

That morning, I trudged my five-foot, four-inch frame up the stairs into our bedroom. Sobbing uncontrollably, I walked inside my closet and collapsed on the white carpet. This time it wasn't about any one thing or two things. There were years and years of pain, hurt, and betrayal gushing out of me all at once. I'm pretty sure my medication added to my descent, but the problems came *before* the medication. Long before. The medication was needed because carrying what I had was no longer manageable. It was unnaturally dark, and I was completely unarmed because I had displaced my faith.

What facade have you been hiding behind so that you can manage and appear to be OK?

CHAPTER 4

THE DIFFERENCE BETWEEN US

Every individual has a distinct history. Just as our DNA is different, those with mental health problems, such as depression, are affected in various ways within different environments: occupational, education, social connections, family dynamics, or other significant areas of functioning. The reasons for depression, responses, and treatments are not the same for everyone. Sure, some issues may fall under the same umbrella, but how you deal with it, well— *that's up to you.* Experience causes some to have a more severe reaction to situations than others.

Growing up in a home with my twin brothers and parents, I could see how each of us had a personal perspective and outcome to our lives even though we were all from the same home. Our relationships and interactions are viewed from our own lens. And our emotional well-being stemmed from those relationships. I was the eldest child by five years. I witnessed more and was privy to more of the truth about my parents; therefore, I had a different perspective and opinion than my brothers. And I'm grateful that they don't share mine. But in the end, each of us made choices that affected our outcome, and so did others. Our risk factors and protective factors were also dissimilar. The little things can change the trajectory of someone's life to a critical degree.

I knew what brought me to the point that I was having a breakdown. I was well aware. I didn't have the strength to press the brakes and stop it. My childhood experiences contributed largely to my being an adult in a sweatshirt and leggings on my closet floor, crying in a way I never had before. At the same time, my incredibly beautiful family was downstairs, utterly unaware of how much I'd been shouldering. No one has a window into anyone's life to see what's still there or the turmoil that's boiling. We don't know; therefore, we shouldn't judge. At times that means we can't stop a person's pain from boiling over, so turning up the heat and making it worse doesn't help.

When I began my relationship with Michael, he was familiar with my familial baggage. I grew up in an emotional environment, and many times it was overdone—highly dramatic. If Michael was going to call me his wife, he needed to know my history. So I told

him everything before we married. My husband
was amazing, but he couldn't possibly understand what had brought me to this point because
of his own level of strength and resilience. He
didn't judge me or make me feel weak. But
Michael couldn't grasp what depression was
doing to his wife; he wasn't able to connect to
the depths of my pain.

Just because you marry someone, it doesn't
mean you know everything about one another,
but you may inherit that history. Whether it
will manifest in problematic issues is something
time reveals. Some assume pain, depression, and
the inability to cope are associated with weakness; that's not necessarily true. With anxiety
and depression as prevalent as it is—affecting
people in ways others wouldn't imagine—do
you really think we are all just weak? Depression
is a leading cause of disability. It's crippling.
Years of keeping my schedule full and staying
busy kept me from seeing or feeling what had
been there all along and how bad it had become.
Being imprisoned with myself caused me to
discover that *I* was empty. Although our experiences and pain are the sum of our reality and

truths, somehow I had to learn how to leave the past behind and focus on my life before it was too late.

Is there something you need to leave behind to improve your well-being?

***

Being a pastor's daughter was rough for me. It wasn't because of the religion, the rules, and working in the church one Sunday after the next. It was because of the lies. The environment was abusive for Mom and it trickled down to creating a hefty batch of emotional damage for me. I had spent most of my life trying to be what I was told to be, which resulted in me having a breakdown. I didn't have a healthy relationship with my father, but many people don't. Mom was dealing with the residue after twenty-eight years of marriage to Dad, and now that they'd been divorced for nearly thirteen years, it was apparent to me that for her, those thorns were still in her just as they were in me. I had difficulty accepting that God was OK with Dad's affairs, lying, and showing disrespect for women in the name of the Bible. The church had been growing and it was a business, so he ran it one way and his family another. That truly weighed on me. Does it mean this is the experience of every pastor's daughter or son? Of course not. But it was mine. And even with therapy and medication, I wasn't able to reconcile with my past. It was still my present and it appeared that it would always be my future.

I needed something else.

Speaking and writing books was my subtle way of telling others not to do what I had done. I didn't want them to fake it; I wanted them to seek authenticity. I wanted people to stop hiding their pain to appease others, not to be bound to their history, so I wrote *Be Free. Be You.* I wanted them to feel free to be authentic, so I wrote *Authentic You.* I wanted young girls, and young people in general, to be what I wasn't, because I knew if they did that they wouldn't be where I ultimately ended up—on the closet floor with tears staining their face, with mangled thoughts and feelings of hopelessness.

I had to own the decisions I'd made. I should have forgiven Dad and let it go. That may have prevented me from carrying everything for as long as I had. Dad had moved on. Mom had moved on. My brothers had moved on. Now it was time for me to ask God to give me the strength to do the same. This was no longer about my father or my childhood.

It was about no one other than me.

★★★

Sobbing uncontrollably, I cupped my hands over my face and begged, "God, I have leaned on everything I can lean on—my husband, my therapist, and my psychiatrist. I didn't want to lean on you. I was told to look at you as a heavenly Father, and I know your words. I have a father, but he wasn't there for me, and he was the first example of a male that I had. I don't trust you because I don't trust any man. That's the problem, Lord," I admitted, sobbing even harder. "I don't trust you. That's the problem I had with Michael. I don't trust anything that looks like a man."

On the floor, with purely unbridled emotions, crying, I curled into a ball. I had no peace. In my mind, I'd leaned over to see what was over the edge and blustery winds just took me. Well, maybe I jumped. But either way, I went off that precipice into the darkest hole I'd ever been in. I had *never* experienced anything so formidable. I never knew precisely how much pain I was grappling with until then. I thought I was strong enough to manage, but it broke me. I didn't think I'd ever make it out of there.

I'd been crying so long that the carpet where I had buried my face was soaked. The only thing I thought to do was pull my phone out of my pocket and play a worship song by Sarah Reeves. I played the same song repeatedly, allowing it to resonate with my needs as it penetrated my soul a little deeper each time. That song was significant because I was at my breaking point. I thought, *None of the things I have going on in my life is more important than getting back to that place with God,* and I completely surrendered. I had nothing left to

offer and was void of physical strength when I
started singing. Only then did I feel a peace and
sense of belonging enveloping me like a warm
blanket. My tears were still flowing when I realized the problem was that I'd been spinning my
wheels, running from God. I finally acknowledged, "I'm not running from you. I'm running
from my dad. I don't want that version of you. I
want *you*."

I had to navigate my way through the
darkness with minimal resources. It was as if my
faith were in its infancy. I had alienated myself
from the one thing that grounded me—my faith
in God—and having done that felt like death.
It was so bad I remember thinking, *I don't know
how I'll get out of this. There is no way I'm going to
be able to escape this.* But that song was my way
of communicating to God—and God illumi-
nated the cave.

A few years ago, something similar
happened. I had an anxiety breakdown that
thrust me into a debilitating state of unrest.
It was more of a physical manifestation than
mental anguish, but it was severe. I was jittery,
had an upset stomach, and couldn't eat.

....

**None of the things
I have going
on in my life is
more important
than getting
back to that
place with God.**

....

Adrenaline surged through my system, prohib-
iting me from calming my mind or body. I'd
been plagued with forty-eight-hour bouts of
insomnia and recurring panic attacks. It was a
rough period, but one that felt entirely different
from this depression.

I call anxiety and depression sisters because
I usually didn't have one without the other. But
the anxiety was triggered by COVID-19, which
triggered the depression. The complexity of a
dual diagnosis is what made it a bit tricky for me
to be treated. I was unseen—invisible to people
once depression took center stage in everything.
No one could continue to handle it because
they weren't trained to do so. The sadness,
hopelessness, loss of interest in doing anything,
crying, emptiness, worthlessness . . . and the
darkness was overwhelmingly opaque as if there
were no sun. I ran the gamut of symptoms.

I don't remember feeling anything like this
at any other point in my life, but what's worse
is that it's common. It's a serious medical illness
that affects one in fifteen people—and the
statistics are continually rising. I'm not alone and
neither are you. Our personality, biochemistry,

genetics, and environment are all risk factors
and contributors to depression. But when you're
going through it, you really aren't sitting there
assessing the cause or whom the breadcrumbs
lead back to; you're praying that you can make
it through that bout. Your only thought is to
survive—*or not*. Before you get to that precipice,
sure, you feel the makings of your life breaking
into a million pieces. That's the breakdown.

Some people with depression may get tired
of talking about what they're going through.
I did. Others may appreciate the opportunity to talk about it. But when you live with
someone, you can go through these episodes
time and time again, so the synopsis remains
the same. Explaining what I was going through
only caused more stress because I was repeating
myself. I felt unheard and misunderstood, and
it seemed to me that people hoped the depression would just one day vanish. The severity
was minimized.

When you tell someone that you're experiencing low-grade depression and they ask why,
sometimes there isn't a clear answer. Sometimes
it's just the situation or something isn't aligning

....

**I'm
not alone
and
neither are you.**

....

correctly. But when my husband or mother asked, "What's wrong?" I didn't always know the answer. It can be difficult to tell others because you don't want to deal with the questions on top of the depression. I was depleted of my mental energy; it was drained from me, which had an adverse effect. My mind continually ruminated on the past, the future, the what-ifs, and it became tiresome. Asking, "What's wrong?" adds to the pressure, and it can make someone feel even more alone—and I feel alone a lot. When I'm anxious or depressed, I try to focus my thoughts on one thing to keep from falling into the darkness. When I don't, it builds and builds until I can't carry one more straw.

But this time the culprit was different. It felt as though I were trying to make my way through an unfamiliar cavern without the sound of dripping water or a slight draft of air alluding to an opening. There was no indication of light, and invisible ankle weights slowed my pace. Everything that could hold me back was in motion. The weights on my ankles were my past. I kept trying to release the weights to get them off me, but I couldn't manage to navigate in the darkness. I couldn't feel the walls. No, it was pitch-black. My fear brought me and my trembling knees to the ground.

It became unusually exhausting when I couldn't sleep. I no longer had that period as an escape from the darkness, so I was filled with hopelessness and remained restless 24-7. Life was utterly *unbearable*. Those were the days I thought about dying. Depression is both a mental and physical weight. It can make you so exhausted that you can lose functionality. Although fatigued, I couldn't sleep. When I lay down all I saw were these incredibly dark moments from my past. They were frightening because they weren't in black and white, like decades-old memories; they were as vivid as when they'd happened—in color. I was living with thoughts of what I wished I had, what I should have done, why I didn't leave, and the verbal abuse that came—it didn't seem it would end. When you suffer from depression, those are the things you are met with. A combination of circumstances aggravate the event itself and depression strikes like the perfect storm. The response varies for everyone.

That day I was in the closet for two or three hours. During that time my daughter came into my room and found me. She asked sweetly, "Mommy, are you OK?" Barely able to lift my head, I nodded as I wiped my tear-stained eyes with my sleeve. "Why are you on the floor in your closet?" she continued.

"I was talking to God," was the only thing I could say. That's what I was doing.

When I finally pried myself off the floor and out of the closet, I went downstairs. Michael said, "I came upstairs and heard you listening to your music. I thought you were praying and worshipping God. Are you OK?"

Again I nodded.

I was ashamed to tell anyone that I was doubting God. I have been devout in my faith except for a few times in my teens. I was a worship leader for years. Family and friends knew it, and that's how people identified me. And that's why I was ashamed. I was saying, "God, if you're real I need you to heal my memories. Take these memories out of my brain and put good ones in it."

When I went off the precipice of mental health that day, I ended up in that cave for two months. Physically, I continued to ensure my children were settled and everything at home was OK, which took tremendous effort. I literally felt like I was having an out-of-body experience similar to when people talk about dying and their spirit lifts from their body. I, too, could see everyone in the room, but I couldn't communicate. Instead, I waded lifelessly through my normal routine in a brain fog, with their conversations and dialogue distant and barely audible, like being underwater. Never have I felt anything so unfamiliar. How was I crying but numb? Again, I couldn't feel and I wasn't sad. Normally tears are associated with sadness or joy. I felt neither, but still I was crying.

The inability to feel is terrifying. Feeling is how you know you're alive. That's life—the highs and lows, pain and joy, happiness and sadness. It's a mixed bag of contrasting things. Even though we hate the pain and the sorrow, and we love the joy and happiness. The thing that makes life go round is the experience of both. When you're numb, you're not living; you

are the walking dead. The logic behind what
I felt was, *If this is what living is like for me, and
I'm unable to feel, I don't want this.* Who would?
This is why some people harm themselves—
they want to feel *something.* They have impulsive
behaviors that give them some temporary pain
or pleasure just to feel something other than
depression. That's why they do it, and that's why
they get hooked. They've been numb for so long
that they feel dead inside.

After running my normal routine I'd return
to the abyss, when in my reality, I hadn't left it.
Michael didn't know what was going on with
me because he had adapted to this version of
me, but Mom knew I wasn't the same—she
was able to discern that I wasn't even close to
being myself.

When I had started treatment with the
psychiatrist, I had been optimistic; I didn't know
another breakdown was on deck. I shared with
Mom that I was glad to get an appointment to
meet with someone in pharmacology because
that's when my medicine changed. She asked
how the new medication was working. Being
completely transparent, I told her I had extreme

agitation, morbid thoughts, I wasn't sleeping, and I was going through withdrawal. She was visibly concerned about me, and, since she is spiritual, she went into prayer for me and my mind—that I would adjust. Beholden to depression, unfortunately, before I got better, I got worse. Mom noticed that, too, and her alarm about my morbid thoughts grew. But I don't think she knew what to do either. Mom was so afraid that she cried. She was scared that I would hurt myself or leave because of the things I was texting and saying to her. I told her, "I feel so horrible, I don't think I'm going to get out of this. I'm no good."

Mom asked, "Why? What happened? Do you need anything?" My clouded eyes struggled to continue reading her text. "You have me," she added. "I'm always here for you. I'll come over and help you with the kids." She's great with the kids, but at that time, my children were probably the only ones who could snap me out of my desperation because they made me feel the most normal. I didn't want to be away from them.

Mom and I continued to communicate, but even then I took a dive and I began ruminating on things in the past. This was dangerous in that state because I'd spiral further and lash out at her with resentment that she had not protected me from Dad—and that turned into anger.

I told her, "No one cares about me. Not even you." That one thought became twenty different thoughts, and I went down twenty different paths. Some people with depression fight a battle that is misunderstood. I say this because if you don't have depression you are most likely to see it the way you understand it.

Initially, when I'd ended up in that cave, there was a little light behind me. But as I ventured further, the light became smaller until the cave was closed off. There was no light to find the path out of there, and it looked as though everything had to get really, really bad before it could get better. As anticipated, the further I went in the cave, the worse it got with every step. Depression is horrible, and I was grieving my history.

I was stunned by the downward progression. By the fourth week, I was in the abyss; it was endless and frightening. I thought I was done,

but somehow I kept praying. When I reached
week five and then six, while lethargic, I felt I'd
gone incredibly far, and finally, *finally*, I saw a
speck of light. Then that speck of light began to
expand, which made me think I might be able
to make my way out of that cave. I kept reaching
for something to grab onto, and, just as I lost
all hope, I felt God lifting me. Sometimes we
need help getting up, and this time I couldn't
do it alone.

The process of getting out of the abyss
seems to take so long because you can feel lost
or stuck. Then you question whether you want
to continue trying. All you think you can do
is stay in the abyss and just die there or inch
toward the hope that you were hanging on to.
I think at that point, for people like me who
struggle from depression, that's where the decision lies. Making it out of the abyss doesn't end
depression—it ends that episode.

Some people say it's a choice. When you
suffer from depression—and I mean, *suffer*—it's
not a choice. Who would choose this? For me,
it's my genetics and experience. All the drama
and shit everyone dropped on me were not *my*

I kept reaching
for something
to grab onto,
and, just as
I lost all hope,
I felt God
lifting me.

choices. However, we need to take ownership of the way we respond and what we choose to do with it all. Will we stay in the depths or keep moving?

I knew I'd caused Michael to suffer along with me. He didn't suffer the same way I did, but, in his own way. He explained that it was difficult because he was cleaning up everyone else's messes. He didn't just get *me* when we married: he inherited all the dysfunction, trauma, clutter, and the results of those. It's hard when you don't know the person you married had these issues. And although I told him as much as I could about my past, I could not have predicted that I'd be dealing with this either.

Over time, things continued to improve. Happiness and laughter showed up, only they were short lived and the melancholia still loomed. He's shown me that marriage is for better or for worse. Michael committed to what he didn't know—and he's still here. When someone has depression, you don't know what you're getting because *they* don't always know.

I wanted someone other than a psychiatrist or therapist to understand and validate that what I'd been through was insurmountable, at times utterly debilitating, and to completely understand what I was fighting . . . and losing to. But over time, with growth, I managed to comprehend that my expectations were too unrealistic. I expected that Michael should know what to say and do when I had those periods of depression. He's my husband—he should be perceptive enough to know why I feel what I feel and what triggered each bout of anxiety or depression, right? That's what I thought or hoped. In reality, I was setting myself up for failure because it wasn't possible for him to identify with or know how to handle mental illness.

Michael is an expert in basketball; he isn't an expert when it comes to anxiety or depression, and not many are. It takes years of studying, testing, working with clients, and so much more to get to the level of comprehension that I needed. Only a licensed professional was capable of understanding and helping me navigate through those moments. The difference between us is that I was experiencing the depression, but

Michael wasn't capable of making sense of the *why* behind everything, especially when there were things I didn't understand or was in the process of learning about depression.

At times we expect people to respond according to our feelings and needs or have the same degree of empathy that we have in similar situations. Again, that isn't a healthy approach, and it can be incredibly unfair, but we don't always accept that perspective when we are in it.

Do the people closest to you know you are battling depression? If so, are they aware of the depth of it?

CHAPTER 5

DEPRESSION IS A LIAR

Where do I go from here?

After several weeks of the deepest, darkest depression, I had to make necessary changes: in medication, rebuilding my relationship with God, and in my approach to life. The depression wasn't going away, but it was manageable if I was honest about where I was on the scale. Making it out of that cave didn't imply I was automatically healed. Someone turning a corner doesn't mean they're back to normal. That means they are trying, so give them support and space to heal. It took years to amass those problems, and it would take time to undo them, but what it meant is that *depression is a liar!*

Have you ever had someone look you in your eyes and lie to you, but you didn't know it at the time? You believed them because they were convincing. Well, depression will do that to you.

Depression made it seem as though I wasn't strong enough to survive, everything was impossible, I was worthless, and no one understood or cared. I questioned the point of life. But I discovered that's what faith, therapy, and the

....

**Making it out
of that cave
didn't imply I was
automatically
healed.**

....

proper medication is for—to prove that life is worth living. There isn't one path or one way to improve your mental health, but I kept searching until I found one that worked for me—and that too may change. Your recipe may be different from mine, and that's fine as long as you work to find it. Life is worth the effort.

In the beginning when I wasn't feeling myself, I knew I was some distance from where I should be. While struggling to sustain my routine and appearance of normalcy, I knew I was heading in the wrong direction. I thought I had a strong network so I sent a text to those close to me while sitting and crying my eyes out. I asked why I felt like this and if it was because I was about to turn forty. I probably would have accepted anything for a response—this level of depression was new to me. I don't think anyone had the right words to say, but I only needed someone to say something I could believe or accept to make me believe I could get through it. We're told when you are going through depression, we should reach out to someone. But can you imagine the outcome if people with depression, substance abuse, alcoholism, a gambling addiction, or anything are reaching out to the wrong resources? I reached out and some of my friends responded, but they weren't helpful. A few of them tried to be relatable, apologized for what I was going through, and asked if I needed anything or if I needed to talk. I asked them if I was normal. I had never gone through anything like this so I didn't know. If that wasn't a sign something was wrong with me, I don't know what else may have been.

The first interaction I had since the pandemic lockdown was with three people who attended my fortieth birthday. When I explained what I was feeling, they each told me, "I'm here." Coming over during COVID-19 was a big deal to begin with, and I appreciated the company as much as the depression allowed. They brought champagne, balloons, and flowers to celebrate. It was really sweet, but sad because I was on the decline. Others tried to spiritu- alize a lot, and given how I was raised, they just confused me even more. A few of my friends discussed what was going on with them without going anywhere near my situation, even though

I asked for help and guidance about what I should do. I was transparent about my diagnosis.

Even when it was visibly apparent that I was struggling, with heavy bags weighing beneath eyes pink from crying, their buyout was to gently ask how I was doing, knowing I would say, "I'll be OK." Then it quickly became a moot issue. Sometimes people choose to play things down so they don't have to intervene. I was so ashamed and scared of my morbid thoughts, I didn't tell anyone how bad they were until I got past them. It's hard to admit that to anyone, let alone my husband. When you have those thoughts it's easy for someone to advise you to talk to someone, but if you are worried about stigma or fear of being judged, you won't speak about it. When I got to the point of complete worthlessness, I refused to let anyone see me. I looked sick; my complexion was grayish—I didn't look the same because I wasn't. On one hand, I wanted someone to *see* me, but they didn't want to see me.

Depression can make you lose hope, faith, and sight of everything. One of the first things I had to acknowledge to survive that episode is that there *is* light, and that's where you will find hope—on the other side of depression. I couldn't see it until I got within range, but I'm here now.

Expectations had a lot to do with my fall, so I decided to invest in people who matter to me. I did that by learning to adjust my expectations. I realized that not everyone was willing to be open and honest and tell me how they really felt. When people go through challenging times in their lives, it doesn't mean they won't be a complete asshole rather than tell you they're struggling. Being vulnerable is tough. Not everyone is willing or ready to take the mask off and let you in or show up in the world as who they are. But I knew I needed to do that, and it was during that period of lockdown with COVID-19 that I learned the most—about myself and others.

I couldn't keep living in the past, hoping for a different result from Dad. It wasn't his fault. He is who he is and he may not want to change. But I can. People have always been able to count on me; when I give you my word, it's done. When someone doesn't honor their word,

**Expectations
had a lot to do
with my fall,
so I decided
to invest in
people who
matter to me.**

it hurts. Since depression tries to take everything it can from you, make sure you have a network of people or a support system you can count on who are invested in helping you get the help you need before those episodes become unmanageable. If you don't have such a network, work toward creating one. It may take time to connect with people who care about you, but don't be disappointed or devastated if your network is empty for a while. That will give you a clean slate so you can be selective and add the right people to it. Having people around who will only disappoint you will contribute to the stress and everything else that's already there. Learn to be OK with situations that are ultimately healthier. It's OK to be alone. Flowers grow out of volcanic ash—you'll survive.

I had a couple of friends whom I believed genuinely cared for me, but even in that, I didn't think they could understand and deal with what I was going through. Is that their fault? Of course not. At the time that was a tough pill to swallow but in hindsight I can't control how others react to situations, a crisis, or to me. Neither can you. People have issues that we

....

If you don't have such a network, work toward creating one.

....

don't know anything about. Some have selfish tendencies or a lack of compassion, and you can't control that either. The bottom line is you can only control what you can manage, and that is *you*. Everyone dealt with COVID-19, which was a crisis. And what did people do? They took steps to keep themselves and their loved ones safe, and COVID-19 showed me who truly cared about me during my crisis.

When I found myself deep in depression, I felt that I had nothing to offer. People who care about you will see clearest when you aren't yourself and this doesn't wane. They won't run or hide. It's not easy, and not everyone can handle it, but depression can bring out a lack of authenticity—and fast. It's OK. It was bound to happen.

When I could no longer conduct business due to COVID-19, friendships changed. We weren't going out, laughing and eating, but the conversation became real. Some of my friends never once called to check on me, but I shouldn't have expected it because those same individuals had never done that before; I just hadn't wanted to see it. Now I had to because

God was working on a major renovation of my life. He was starting with me and working his way through my connections. The hardest part was surrendering to it, but I did; and then I got to the point where I stopped wanting to know what had happened to my friends who had fallen off the radar.

You have to expect that change happens every day. People will come and some will go, and that is a normal progression of life. It's not unusual; it's seasonal, and some friends are conditional. Sometimes we don't pay attention to the people we let into our network. And just because they're in doesn't denote that they fully understand us—or anxiety and depression. Maybe there's a time stamp on some friendships. Again—that's OK. It's normal to lose friends, and it doesn't mean that none of them was ever real friends. It indicates a shift, telling you things have changed. Accept it. I lost a lot of friends. But I've realized my worth and what they lost from me.

Depression can thwart the way you view things, and you may blame it on other people's inability to cope with your illness. Whether that's true or not, it happens; when you choose to move on you will begin to heal a lot faster. Seasons change. Leaves fall off trees, but a few months later, new, beautiful leaves grow at the beginning of another season. You will have many new seasons. Trying to figure everyone out or understand every situation can be daunting and damaging. We're meant to let go of a lot of things, but life should never be one of them.

Feelings of abandonment aren't limited to those people with anxiety, depression, or some form of mental illness. People are human beings with emotions; thus they feel. The difference is that their triggers may be different and their responses may vary. Some of us with depression may feel abandonment with a greater degree of intensity. For others it can seem like the end of the world. My depression ran the gamut of abandonment, sadness, feeling invisible, and feeling that no one cared enough to hear my desperate pleas for help. Naturally, we want people to genuinely care.

But again, I couldn't control anyone's actions toward me and I had to stop trying. Sometimes, no matter how hard we try, we can't make people understand what we are going through. It seems nearly impossible to the untrained ear and eye. Under those circumstances, I found that the best thing to do was to use the lifelines and resources that existed. If that takes you outside of your network to a professional—then go there. The key is that when seeking help from a professional psychiatrist or therapist, they see you. They are trained to understand you, hear you, and guide you toward better insight, and help you build your own toolbox. That could help you be more proactive rather than reactive and keep you ahead of the anxiety and depression episodes. Don't underestimate that option. Ask questions to ensure you are working with the professional who is right for you.

There is good and bad anxiety; I had to acknowledge that I wasn't going to allow my bad anxiety to control me. I became exhausted, constantly analyzing the devastation of a past I couldn't fix or change. I gave it too much power and authority. I canceled out a lot of the noise of what everyone was telling me I should do and got back to the root of trusting and believing what God was putting in me. My intuition was correct. All of that contributed to initiating my healing. Make no mistake, I continued with therapy and cognitive behavioral therapy (CBT) techniques, and I adjusted to my new medication. I looked forward to seeing more of the good things in life while enjoying and appreciating Michael and the love of my children.

Moving forward, I've worked hard to focus on the people who deserve me to be at my best and things that are beneficial to my well-being. My relationships with God, myself, my husband, and my children are at the top of that list. This change comes from a true understanding of oneself, and it is so much richer and sweeter than it was four years ago when I had a breakdown. Since then, I have learned a great deal, and I'm still learning.

Life is precious and we're only given an unspecified period in which to enjoy it. I realized that I needed to give my energy to the things that are most important. I've learned how to be compassionate with myself by eliminating talking to myself in a negative way. I'm not perfect, but I am recovering, which is a continual process. I treat myself gently as I shepherd myself into the right frame of mind. I try not to spend hours and days beating myself up because I went backward. Instead, I acknowledge that it will happen. I stopped telling myself that any progress I'd made meant nothing because I went backward for a moment. That's not true.

I've slowed down and started living in the moment, which keeps me from setting myself up for anxiety or depression. That's how I stay grounded. I try not to talk about negative things unless the purpose is to address an issue. We have the propensity to project what we reflect on, which can send us to the past to dwell on it. When I thought I had processed or gotten over something but continued to bring it up or talk about it with multiple people, without any purpose, it was a sign that I had not properly processed it. It doesn't mean I will never fall again, but it does mean I know how and where to get the help I need before reaching that precipice.

With depression, it's necessary to have a solid game plan when things don't feel right. Internalizing everything to appear outwardly strong and together will ultimately make it worse. We can't fake being OK forever, and that's not a role anyone currently in my life asked me to play. We assume we are supposed to be OK all the time, which isn't our reality.

In the past, whenever I heard people talk about depression, even though I had anxiety and depression, I didn't know it could be like this. I'd never in my life fallen off the precipice of mental health. And when it happened, I had to ask myself, *Is this what people mean when they're talking about being depressed?* Being lost in solitude presented time for several uncomfortable realities to compound and hit me at once—family, abandonment, history, and everything in between.

Growing up, I saw and experienced what children should not, and when you see something you can never unsee it. Seeing it is not the issue; it's being accountable for what you see and then addressing it properly. This was the time to address what I saw—about myself. I dug in and started asking myself some rather difficult questions. *Am I comfortable with my truth? What have I learned? What am I attracting? Whom am I*

attracting? What am I willing to accept at this age?
What am I still dealing with that I should not be?
What patterns do I need to break that I haven't?

Then I had to go to work and make the
necessary modifications.

I had the right balance of the proper medication and therapy. Just because you are placed
on a specific prescription by a doctor, that
doesn't guarantee it's the right one or that it
will be effective for you long-term. I had to
change medications. Unfortunately, sometimes
the only way they find out what's best for you
is through trial and error. If it's not working,
don't force it; speak up. Doctors, therapists, and
psychiatrists only know what you tell them.
Besides medication, a big part of my healing was
reflecting and answering these questions while
God was holding the mirror in front of me. He
was showing me I could get through this, but I
had to acknowledge some gigantic truths, and at
the same time not allow depression to swallow
me. God was meeting me where I was—in the
darkest of places—saving me, from me.

What truths do you have to acknowledge
and reconcile?

CHAPTER 6

A LITTLE SELF-REFLECTION AND SELF-CARE

One of the things I know how to do well is take care of others, and I took care of other people better than I did myself. I didn't realize it initially, but most of the time, despite all the care I gave to others, there was no self-care on my list. That leaves the questions, *Who is taking care of me?* and, *What happens when you don't take proper care of yourself?* Why is it so difficult for women to pause long enough to get what they need for their well-being, which allows them to better take care of others?

When I was in that place, I should never have contemplated driving myself to the hospital. Sometimes I feel that I have to be as drastic as going to check myself into a hospital in order for people to take me seriously and check on me. The disheartening part is that it's not an act; it's where I legitimately am during a crisis. When people are used to seeing you manage your way out of difficult situations, survive challenges and painful moments, and on top of that help others, they see you as a survivor. They think you will manage to survive anything and you'll get through it, so they don't have to worry about you. But what if you

··

Who is taking care of me? And what happens when you don't take proper care of yourself?

··

don't? What if that particular time you needed someone to help you? Just because you seem OK doesn't mean you are. Often people still function in certain environments such as the workplace or school. They could be suffering in silence—and people can only withstand so much weight.

When you have a mental health crisis, the best way to rebound is to practice self-care. You can spend your time focusing on everything and everyone else, but that's a sure way to lose your balance. Relationships with people have always been a challenge, even before I met Michael. Michael just added another level to my relationships. When I am in, I'm in, and when I love, I love. I have needed to set boundaries for others, and I consider myself to be safe. I bring honesty and vulnerability; I give my all, my time, my resources—and my friends are your friends. I don't hold anything back. I am selfless. But when I discovered what my network consisted of, I had to look inward and ask myself, *Who is really here to take care of me when I need it?* When I realized I didn't have what I needed, I lost my balance.

Have you ever lost your balance and fallen?

Whew! It took me a long time to admit that, especially as someone who wasn't raised to see herself that way. Even if I am emotionally struggling and someone needs encouragement, I've always been responsive to their needs. I am that go-to person. I have given so much of myself and shared my wisdom with people I care about, as well as total strangers. I've always continued to behave that way, even when I wasn't getting that in return.

The problem isn't who I am, but that I haven't been very kind to myself over the years. When you feel inadequate in some aspects, sometimes you overcompensate by trying to please or help others. And that can wear on you. The things I provided for people close to me were some of the very things I wanted others to provide for me. Oddly, I wasn't taking care of myself or my mental health as well as I could take care of others. I was in that headspace that if I gave a little more, this person would give me what I needed. They would see my needs too.

Nonetheless, the outcome proved incredibly lopsided. I never needed anything material from others, but it was tangible because it would have touched my soul. I needed understanding, acceptance, and a feeling of being loved for who I was and not for what I could do.

Even before I met Michael, people gravitated toward me because I presented myself as a resilient and emotionally strong person. I may have gotten knocked down, but I always found a way to get back up. I think people have tried to gain that strength from me because while I have been mistreated and betrayed, I am not afraid to address and talk about hard things. On the flip side, it didn't mean it didn't hurt me or cause pain. It meant I got back up. It's difficult for me to understand anyone who can live their life knowing there are things hidden under the rug. You know they're there, but you don't try to clean them up. I don't want to hide things, suppress them, or stuff them inside. I don't want you to either. If someone doesn't want to tell me something, I respect that, but if they need me to listen or help, I can do that. But after *this* mental health crisis, I decided to give to myself what I give to other people. If no one comes along, I am learning to be content that I am not lacking. I can provide for myself the things I need the most.

I have committed to knowing what I need and getting it. At the top of my self-care list are *prayer* and *meditation*. That's how I began feeding my soul and pouring into myself what I needed most. You can't heal if you don't recognize what you're lacking. I knew. Through that current of prayer and meditation I was able to begin having true joy and confidence. Emotions and feelings will arise, and I have to be prepared to handle them.

The next thing on my self-care list is *acknowledging without judging* or spending hours ruminating over why I have certain thoughts and feelings. It could be an "aha" moment. And that moment doesn't need to be spent going down a perilous dark hole ruminating about these things; doing less of that is how I stay in a healthy place. When and if that under-standing comes, it comes, but I don't need to make it come. Forcing it can bring about an undesired outcome.

....

You can't
heal if you
don't recognize
what you're
lacking.

....

When something triggers a negative pattern for me, *I write everything that's on my mind in my journal*. It doesn't have to have a rhyme or reason. It can be an obsessive thought about someone else, me, my work, anything. Whatever it is I usually find that it's not as significant as I thought it was and I immediately feel lighter. While I'm writing, initially the negative self-talk repeats itself like a broken record. It's shocking to see how many times I've written those things and that I actually believe them about myself. I have to look outside of myself to see that. Then I realize the people who imparted those thoughts trained me well. I have to let those thoughts come and go like ships passing in the night. Even after all the therapy I've had, I still have those thoughts, but I've gotten better at letting them pass so it doesn't defeat the purpose.

The fourth and final thing on my self-care list is *movement*. Some call it exercising or working out, but I call it movement because I choose whatever way I feel I need to move each day. Studio exercises, Pilates, breathing, I like the challenge of movements and being aware of my body and breath. I've found that just taking thirty minutes or an hour for myself is a game changer regardless of what it does for my body. Some think if they don't see the change, there is no change, but that is not accurate. Those are the things I am starting to take notice of now. What people don't realize is that certain types of thoughts and exercises stress me out when I am obsessing about the calorie burn. I need to do things that relieve stress rather than add to it. I can't enjoy the moments of working out when my mind is fixated on what it's going to do for me. When I'm already worrying about how a workout will change me, it's counterproductive. These exercises help me live in the moment and be present, rather than diving into the past searching for answers. I do what works now. This is helping me translate this behavior into other aspects of my life and emotional well-being.

A healthy routine is necessary, regardless of the self-care activities you choose to engage in. Some say they don't have time to do things for themselves, but if you don't make time to take care of yourself, you may soon be running on empty or feeling burnout. Then you really won't be capable of managing aspects of your life or

··

**If you don't
make time
to take care
of yourself,
you may soon
be running
on empty or
feeling burnout.**

··

be reliable for those you love. It's like a car. If you fill the gas tank and get timely maintenance, it's more likely to keep running for a long time. However, if you neglect it, it'll only be useful for so long. Make an investment in yourself and your well-being for the long run.

Do you have a self-care routine? If so, what helps you create balance in your life?

CHAPTER 7

A TAILORED PROTOCOL TO KEEP YOU HEALTHY

I wish there were a magic pill that all of us who suffer with anxiety, depression, or any form of mental illness could take and be cured, but unfortunately medicine is not one-size-fits-all, and depression certainly doesn't work that way. You have to make sure you're on the right medication and the correct dosage *for you,* that the side effects are minimal, and that it works without doing more damage in the process. Sometimes you have to be prepared to go through adjustments to get it right.

There are a lot of moving parts when it comes to receiving the right treatment. If you are someone who needs medication and decides to take it, know that medication alone is not enough. I have been around a lot of people who are on medication. While they take their medicine, that's all they've done and that alone may not fix the problem. What I've learned is that people have to make lifestyle changes as well, and at times, they are substantial. You can't go into treating depression thinking, *I am going to take this pill and in six to eight weeks I'll be brand-new.* No, that will help get your chemicals right—dopamine, norepinephrine, and serotonin—but there are reasons why you fell into the depression and your anxiety is exacerbated. Yes, there are physiological and biological factors but also situations, the way you are brought up, experiences, trauma and the like that contribute to those biological factors. If those reasons still exist, so do the problems. The history may be so incredibly profound that the trigger still exists. The right medication can help the chemical imbalance but doesn't fix the fact that we cannot change history.

Long before I knew I had a diagnosis and agreed to take medicine on a regular basis, I would just sit and talk in therapy—working to unravel that history. I did that for nearly four years before the therapist stumbled upon a diagnosis for me. My therapist thought she would be more effective for me if I went and spoke to my doctor about taking medicine. When I first went to therapy, I thought I was going for somebody else. I held Dad accountable for screwing me up, and growing up in my house contributed to my situation. Because of that, I thought I needed therapy to undo all that mess. But the common denominator in both those scenarios was me.

I found out in therapy that it wasn't for other people—it was *for me*.

I first had a desire to talk to a therapist when I was around twenty-five, but I didn't act on it then because my family was private and didn't agree that I should go. There was a spiritual stigma, along with religious and cultural beliefs that weren't in alignment, and I was taught that doctors don't know what they're talking about, God knows. But since I was getting married and the adverse history had nothing to do with Michael, I thought it would be good to begin removing some of that baggage. I tried to do it in the way I was told the religious world did it—without seeing a psychologist or therapist.

Once we were married and had children of our own, I knew I had to do better. I prayed and asked God to change the way I was parenting my children; it was outside of what I knew, and I needed to change. I decided that I didn't want to send my children to therapy because of me. I didn't want to cause them emotional trauma or pain.

....

**Therapy
wasn't for
other people—
it was for me.**

....

One of the pillars that drew Michael and I together was our faith. When I started therapy at thirty-one, many things were challenged, and it appeared as though what I was learning challenged our relationship, but that's what growth will do. When my belief system was shaken a bit it caused greater anxiety because our relationship was built on our shared faith and religious values. I believed that was one of the things Michael loved most about me. When I reached the point I knew I needed to see a therapist, I was afraid. I wasn't prepared for it to challenge the things I held so dear. I had to take a risk and trust God when I decided to go to therapy. Religion and spirituality were such a huge pillar that it took complete faith in God that my whole world wouldn't come crashing down when that house was shaken. I didn't know what to expect, and it was scary.

I think it is important to talk to someone first before we jump in and start taking medication. It can help us flex our own natural muscles first and see if our condition is situational, biological, due to traumatic events, or all three. In an attempt to handle or adjust to the trauma, you have most likely learned unhealthy habits to manage and cope. Thoughts produce emotions, which result in behaviors, but you can learn to control your thoughts, which can derail maladaptive behaviors. Dialectical behavioral therapy (DBT) focuses on skills acquisition, strengthening, and generalization. You learn certain skills in counseling, strengthen them, and learn to apply them to other areas of your life. Sometimes people don't know how to apply the skills learned in therapy, and this teaches you how to do just that.

The problem is that we wait so long to go to a therapist that by the time people actually reach out for help it's already a crisis situation. If they wait too long, they may lack the patience to go through the process. That can be detrimental. Likewise, when you go through depression or an anxious season it's emotionally and physically draining. You're exhausted because you are trying to do all you can to hold on, not give up, cave, or break. Getting out what is disruptive to you by talking to a therapist is good because you may feel that you can talk to someone who is effectively listening.

I was thirty-one when I finally went to therapy. I was scared to go talk to someone because I was afraid someone would know who my dad was, and I was afraid of embarrassing my family. But my first therapist told me, "There are two things I want you to remember. One, you are the only one in therapy, not your family or friends. Don't leave the office and expect that what you and I are doing together is going to make them change. Two, you're going to come in here and talk to me for forty-five minutes and feel the weight of the world is on your shoulders, and some days you will feel great. But regardless of how you feel after that session, that's when the true work begins."

After that first appointment, I went into therapy with a clear perspective of what I was getting myself into. All my life I'd been taught that the world isn't kind, and I'd been shown that by some of the people in my family. I experienced that at home and when I left the house. But I was born an open, loving, and honest Achea. The conflict between who I was and who I was taught to be was too much. I don't think it was ever a matter of *if* I would break down, it

was of *when*. There was always friction or disso-
nance when I was around my family because I
try to walk in a level of truth and transparency.
When people hide things or would rather not
talk about them, it's an uncomfortable feeling for
me. When I am around people who are inau-
thentic, it does something to me. I am showing
up as who I am and that doesn't change. There's
always a part of me listening to them talk, and I
can recognize when it's not authentic.

I think the way that I started the whole
process at thirty-one is why I had the resolve
to fight through it and keep going. I didn't
start taking medicine until I was almost thir-
ty-five. I hung in there for as long as I could.
During those four years of therapy I was able to
figure out and work through several things, but
a whole new world opened up when I started
taking medication. That was due to the way my
body reacted to stress—it was biological.

In the environment in which I was raised,
my body reacted to stress. Any stress was bad.
Even now my body experiences anxiety symptoms such as heart palpations, racing thoughts,
inability to focus, insomnia, stomach issues,

I don't
think it was
ever a matter
of *if* I would
break down, it
was of *when*.

tremors, or the jitters. I spoke with my doctor, and we have a protocol for it. It is truly my body; it's not anything psychological. And that is the danger of waiting too long to get proper treatment: ultimately it can become a biological problem. I wasn't born like that, but my body remembers the way it coped with stress as a child. My stomach acts up because that's what it did then. Although it doesn't happen as often as it used to, if my body senses anything in my environment potentially dangerous or stressful, it reacts. The same thing happens if your body reacts to allergens or to pollen in nature: it immediately starts to fight, and you get cold symptoms.

Today I still have anxiety flare-ups where my body is in a fight-or-flight mode and my emotional regulation is on high, but my mind isn't. There are occasions when I appear to be perfectly fine, yet I experience physical symptoms that indicate I'm not. When I start sensing the physical sensations of an anxiety attack, which build over time in your system like an allergy attack, I have to address it immediately or people will be able to notice it. Unfortunately, going thirty-one years without therapy caused my body to continue learning unhealthy ways to cope. But now, through therapy, I've developed protocols that help me. Having a proper protocol can help, and it's a distraction from potential triggers.

Part of that protocol is taking care of my sleep. For some with depression, sleep may not come easily, and there are myriad reasons for this. Childhood trauma has caused significant disruption to my sleep pattern. There are times when I wake up with a racing heart in the middle of the night. I've started practicing taking slow, deep breaths, and it helps. I bought a little apparatus called CalmiGo that you blow into and it vibrates. You can put lavender or citrus essential oil in it for a calming effect. When I feel my heartbeat racing, I use it, and it helps. When I lie down and try to rest, I sleep with a weighted blanket, which is also calming. Rather than stay in an uncomfortable state, my first preference is to try natural methods to help me sustain that calmness. Diffusing lavender at night and using a humidifier have noticeable benefits for me. I take small steps that collectively make a big difference. The key is to have a protocol that works rather than do nothing. Find what works for you.

Too often we feel the unease creeping in, but we don't stop and explore natural things that can bring balance. When I began therapy, early in the process I learned to be curious and open myself up to the possibility of healing because I was made aware that I needed it. Doing so led to learning more about myself. Sometimes we think going to therapy will give us the answers to fix the people we think are causing the problem. That's not what therapy is about. Some of those people may be in therapy for their own stuff, while others may not think they did anything wrong. Then there are those who may not care one way or the other. Accepting that was the beginning of crafting a healthier relationship with myself. It kept me focused on what I needed and the changes I could make that were beneficial to me—no one else. Sure, I'm still a work in progress, and it culmi-nated with the breakdown in my closet during COVID-19, but I learned in the worst place I've ever been that there are solutions to finding

a healthy balance. When you hear it does get
better—*it does.*

Understanding my anxiety and depression,
the triggers, and how to process what I am
feeling is like baking a cake, and now it needs to
be iced—which means I'm continually imple-
menting what is beneficial to my overall well-
being. I understood the importance of self-value,
self-worth, and being internally healthy. Going
through those processes when I initially began
therapy got me ready for cognitive behavioral
therapy. For the most part I knew who I was,
what my triggers were, what happened to me,
and what relationships I wanted to have or
didn't have. I told my therapist I needed to learn
how to flex my muscles because I was burned
out. I spaced out my visits to give myself time,
space, and grace. Healing isn't linear. You will
go backward, but over time you will also have
more peaks than valleys. There will be things
that work now that you wouldn't have thought
of doing before.

It took me two weeks to pull it together. I
spent seven successive days going into my closet
crying my eyes out on the floor. Michael let

....

**Healing
isn't linear. You
will go backward,
but over time
you will also
have more peaks
than valleys.**

....

me go through it because there was nothing he could do and, in fact, I told him there was nothing he could do. In the movie *The Shawshank Redemption*, when Andy was wrongfully imprisoned for something he didn't do, he had two choices: to stay in prison or escape. Andy knew there was a better option than accepting that his life would be spent in prison, so he escaped. He dug that tunnel into the sewer and crawled through poop; the smell was terrible and there was hardly any light in that tunnel, but it was a way out that he had to build or create himself.

I want you to understand that sometimes you have to go through the ugliness and the tough parts to make the way for yourself. It isn't anyone else's job to do it for you. But what if where you came from isn't the place you are supposed to be? What if where you came from is the place you lost yourself? Do you start making excuses to justify staying there? No. Create another path.

I created a mental picture of what a new path would look like, but when I tried to follow it, even with the familiar things, I only saw complete darkness. My instincts prompted me to go back to the place that was familiar, although unhealthy. We equate familiarity with safety, but they are not one and the same. I had to use my intuition to lead me out of the darkness into a more enlightened place. Imagine the muscles and strength you're building to fight your way through something. When you climb back up to where you were, you are using the muscles you already had. When you go through to the other side, you are doing something you didn't know was possible. Even though you know what's back there and you're familiar with it, be willing to go to parts unknown when that's no longer what's best for you.

I believed that if I worked my way out of that cave what I would get to on the other side had to be better than where I was. I wanted to create something healthier.

Why do you keep going back to the same place that is causing the pain, anxiety, or depression? Are you ready to create something better that's indicative of who you want to become? What will your new protocol be?

CHAPTER 8

BECOMING YOUR OWN SAFE SPACE

Becoming my own safe space wasn't instantaneous. It took years of undoing the entire foundation that was created for me. I didn't know that language—"safe space." So in the midst of navigating through new territories, mental health concerns, therapy, medication, and rebuilding my faith, I had a huge learning curve. I didn't know that being safe within ourselves was something that we were allowed to consider. Once I realized that it was a possibility and I was an option, I found that I wasn't a safe space. I had to break down my foundation, define it, reconstruct it, and rebuild with the proper materials. Laying a more solid foundation led to greater stability. Therefore, any future renovations will only be small adjustments.

Once I understood what it meant to be a safe space, I recalled that I used to be a safe space at eight, nine, and ten. I felt comfort and solace being alone with my thoughts. They were positive and happy, and I was able to be me. Chaos surrounded me. Anyone and anything else was disruptive. But by twelve years old, I had lost that safe space.

One way I had to rebuild my foundation was to change my perception of how others saw me. Along with the stress that had begun to take its toll, I was called fat, a crybaby, too sensitive, nonathletic, and told my head was too big. I was instructed not to be too curious or ask questions about sex. If I did, I was promiscuous. Laughing and giggling were silly and stupid. "Don't be a stupid, silly girl. Be serious about your business," was a common message. After trying to appease my father by becoming more composed and austere, I was told that I took myself too seriously. By then, I started believing the negative and hurtful things my father and people in the church said about me until I finally accepted that they must be true. I internalized what my father and other adults said and how they perceived me—even though I knew they didn't really see me. But I couldn't change them.

Another step of rebuilding my foundation came by establishing my core beliefs. Sometimes people think you have to hear things repeatedly before they affect you, cause you to question who you are, or see how others view you. Although I heard criticisms from my dad often,

it was actually the first time I heard them that
caused the most damage. Then the misogy-
nistic patriarchal stuff that was force-fed to girls
followed. It's easier to stay unenlightened and
uninformed. Many of the things I was taught
as a child, especially as it pertained to religion, were intentionally biased and destructive.
After experiencing years of ongoing damage I
was forced to start from zero, without building
instructions—researching, learning, experiencing, conversing, and rediscovering what I
truly believed in and establishing my core beliefs.

Finally, I had to create a new, strong foundation by keeping only the people in my life
who would support me. Starting from scratch
prompted me to show up to life raw and vulnerable so I could determine my truest friends. It
was difficult for me, but openness was necessary if I was to learn new things and adopt a
better way of being, loving, and living. Once I
unlearned those embedded negative thoughts
and behaviors and removed all the junk, like an
archaeology dig, I went deeper and cleared out
people. It wasn't easy because they were people
I genuinely cared about or loved. I didn't have

any hard feelings or remorse, and I didn't do it in anger, yet it was necessary solely as a survival tactic. Now that I had a lot more room in my life, I could fill that space with light and what I truly thought and believed.

Removing thoughts, perceptions, ideologies, and shit from others will allow you to see what you need to see. It gave me the space to fill my life with what brings me joy, comfort, safety, and healing. Yes, I needed a place to heal, and this process of becoming my own safe space gave me that.

I made a wish list of how I wanted to show up in the world and who I wanted to be for myself, my husband, and my children. In the process of decluttering my life and discarding unhealthy core beliefs, I saw how damaged I was. The individual I wanted to be and how I cared for myself would impact how I treated my family and the friends I had left. I knew I couldn't be anything to anybody without becoming what I needed to be to me first.

I wanted to get back to that little girl who was in the room at eight, nine, and ten years old before the debilitating and life-changing labels were imposed. I wanted to get to the place where I was woke, smart, and understood the dynamics of people without being jaded. I didn't want to be as serious as I had been, and I wanted to be that safe space for myself. A great deal of my journey has been about recovering that person and working to regain what I've lost—*my innocence*—which is something that should never be taken from anyone.

In this process, there were a whole lot of mistakes. I didn't get it quite right but it wasn't for lack of trying. The first and second times I tried to become my own safe space, I was still attempting to become this superwoman and wonderful person to other people before being nice and kind to myself. I needed what I was giving, but at the time, giving seemed to help a little bit, until it didn't work anymore. What was missing was still missing, and I hadn't embraced the concept of putting myself first. My breakdown during COVID-19 happened, adding to my struggles.

I made several mistakes—did a lot of undoing and redos, but I finally figured it out

A great deal of my journey has been about recovering that person and working to regain what I've lost— my innocence— which is something that should never be taken from anyone.

and got it right. Although I wanted to quit, I refused. It took work in more than one area, but now, although I'm still learning, everything is clear, and I understand what happened and the why behind it. Sometimes I won't reach the why, and learning to accept that is pivotal. Developing resilience is a critical aspect of our well-being. If we don't learn to navigate adverse history in a healthy manner, we are inviting it to affect our most treasured safe space—our thoughts and frame of mind—because they shape the way we feel. And if we experience a distressing or traumatic event, the likelihood of developing post-traumatic stress disorder (PTSD) increases, especially after prolonged occurrences.

I have decluttered my brain of all the religious beliefs I was not in agreement with, as well as various toxic relationships—everything that had built up over time that contributed to the damaged Achea. I went in and renovated with the biggest hammer I could swing! I tore it all down to bare bones and did a remodel. It sucked to see what was inside me and feel that surge of pain spill out when the walls crumbled down—it felt incredibly raw and painful, like a wound that wouldn't heal. But after going *through* the renovation, the wound finally healed. All that remains is a scar; it's a reminder that I made it.

I never thought that becoming your own safe space was a possibility until I participated in eye movement desensitization and reprocessing (EMDR), which is a psychotherapy that allows people to heal from symptoms and emotional distress that come as a result of trauma. It's a specific method of treatment that can help people with trauma reprocess information. It may not be for everyone, but in my quest for healing I was willing to explore other resources and figure out what healing looked like.

When I left the therapist I'd seen for the first seven years of therapy, I sought another therapist who provided treatment using cognitive behavioral therapy. I recall her asking me a question that brought my life into view. She asked, "Who are your safe people?" I gently closed my eyes and acknowledged them by replying, "Michael. You. And the lady I am working with for my eating disorder." After looking at her expression, I dropped my head

because that's all I had. The issue wasn't that
I only had three people. My therapist noted
that *I* hadn't made the list. She said, "Achea,
you know it's OK for you to be your own safe
space?" Actually, I didn't. Did you? What's more
jarring than realizing, in good conscience, that I
couldn't name myself to be my own safe space?
Yup, that's a problem.

When my therapist asked me to identify
the people whom I felt were safe for me to be
with, one criteria I used was that the person
be someone I could be myself around. I didn't
have to lie to just to survive. That "someone"
wouldn't judge me and would accept me for
me. I knew whether I paid them or not, these
were the people who I felt were a safe space. At
the time, I thought it was incredibly disheartening that to feel safe I had to reach into the
network of professionals I'd hired to make me
feel OK. However, that's not an issue anymore.
If that's where it is, and it's working, I'm OK. I
discovered that a person can only become their
own safe space when they acknowledge what or
who isn't.

Having a safe space is where *I* feel safe at all times. Once I realized I wasn't in safe environments or around safe people, I became introverted and quiet. The quarantine caused me to analyze friendships and associations with people, and in doing this I cleared up my schedule too. People may think that's a sign of depression and, yes, I guess you could say the depression made it easier for me to clear my mind, my soul, and my schedule. Whether it's the pandemic that causes you to make changes or something that brings awareness to help you understand your life needs a little clearing out—pay attention because it can make a difference.

Typically, I would try to power through tough situations, but I didn't want to this time. I decided that I didn't have to do that anymore. I wasn't in a happy place. While I was in the cave, the instinctive thing to do was to crawl my way up to where I was justifying my happiness. But then I realized that if I was feeling like this, I couldn't have been happy and that place wasn't what I needed. If I went back the way I came I'd end up where all this began. It wasn't working. I needed to dial it back, focus inward, and focus

....

A person can
only become
their own safe
space when they
acknowledge
what or
who isn't.

....

on my family. I needed to find another way out of that cave because I never wanted to feel that kind of break again.

At the beginning of my breakdown, just before I started going into the closet, I told Michael I needed time to go away and get help. It didn't mean he or our children had caused the problem. They hadn't. They were in the middle of my personal war. Michael thought maybe it was him, and he tried asking me a lot of questions. He was having a hard time understanding where I was, because I didn't understand it myself, nor could I communicate it to him. As much as I love Michael, Michael II, and Ardyn, I had to be on for them when I felt broken inside. *And how do you turn something on that's broken?* But now I find it best to be honest with my family so Michael is better equipped to support me while Michael Jr. and Aryden have a better understanding of what their mother is going through.

In essence, they deserved so much more than what I was able to provide. I deserved more too. But I didn't know how to love the right way, or in a healthy manner, because I didn't love myself. How do you know what love feels like if you don't feel love or loved? My entire experience with love has been transactional. You have to do *this* to get *that*. If you want this—do that. I didn't know.

When I had the conversation with Michael about my mental state, it was a last-ditch effort to communicate what I was feeling before I ended up in pieces on my closet floor. I was at a place of sheer desperation. At that time, it had nothing to do with them, but home was not a safe space. They were there and there was the constant pressure to perform, when I was so broken. I had a lot of responsibilities and roles, but I wasn't whole or even a half—I was a shell of myself. I was inside myself fighting not to give up, but outside of me I was attempting to do all the things I was truly incapable of doing.

What pushed me to keep trying was not wanting to disappoint my husband, children, or anybody else. I wanted to figure it out so I could give them better than what they were getting. I decided to give myself a two-week deadline to lock myself away, cry, meditate, and pray. If I came out of that closet after two weeks of

....

How do you know what love feels like if you don't feel love or loved?

....

praying and crying the same way that I went in, I knew I was checking myself in somewhere.

Although I could only go in the closet intermittently, at that point *my closet was my safe space*. I'd drag myself out of the shower, put on some clothes, get up after two, three, or four hours of crying, and go downstairs to try and stick to my routine. My eyes were red and swollen from crying and my children would look at me as if they were wondering, *Mommy, what's wrong?* I'm sure they were scared. I looked like I had no life in me. It's hard to show evidence of life when you are fighting for it.

Besides the fear of disappointing my husband and children, deep down inside I believed there was more. I'd seen people who were happy. It wasn't because of what people told me; I saw it and I wanted to push my way through this and see if I could get there too. I had hope. It wasn't much, but I had enough. I was determined that if I couldn't help myself, I'd find someone to help, and they could show me the way to getting the mental health care I needed. I knew I didn't have to remain that way forever. Neither do you. Somewhere deep down inside, I still had this fighter mentality. I didn't want to let my childhood win. I believed I could conquer it, and so I went in pursuit of a new lens—and found one.

I created the place that I never had. A safe space is a place with no judgment, complete honesty, and unconditional acceptance. It took a long time for me to discover that place was in me. Getting to a safe space within myself actually helped me see God the right way. I was raised to believe the opposite: you have to see God rightly, then you will see yourself. I needed to get to a good place where I could see myself and put everything into perspective so I could see and feel the presence of God the right way, more clearly. And that's what happened. Now I can see God in the place he deserves to be and the place he is in, in my life. I see things the way *I* am supposed to see them for myself. I know that because of the internal joy and peace I have, which I didn't have before. The chaos had made its way inside. External peace is fleeting, while internal peace can be lasting if it's nurtured and protected. Becoming your own safe space feels liberating and safe.

When you don't have a safe space, it's time to create one because *you* are enough. To me, everyone else is icing on the cake, because—just like you—I am the cake.

I am very intuitive, and I've always felt it. When the thought of other people exiting my life made me feel as though I wouldn't survive, that was evidence that I was not self-reliant or healthy. To base your happiness or validation on what others give you is *unhealthy*. That's one of the reasons I knew I wasn't in a safe space and I was relying on everyone else for stability, or something that I wasn't giving myself. If I had to morph into another person to keep those people in my life, I did my best. When you're in a space that feels like the bottom is going to fall out, it's not safe.

You should not fear your home or any place you go. If you do, you shouldn't be there. At a young age I realized that my home wasn't safe; my safe space was connected to people. Our home environment was volatile and changed abruptly and frequently. Those individuals who comprised my family made "home" an unstable and unreliable place for me to be in too.

....

When you don't have a safe space, it's time to create one because you are enough.

....

Today the home I share with Michael and our kids is my place of refuge. I don't look to people to be my safe space. I look to myself to be my safe space. However, there are other people whom I consider to be safe people. I built an external safe space and started by diving into what makes me happy.

Take a moment and ask yourself what makes *you* happy and work toward cultivating that internally and creating that environment externally. For instance, I'm drawn to white furniture, vibrant green plants, big windows, and lots of natural light. I existed in such darkness for so long that my soul hungered for the light, both inside and out.

Can you recognize your safe space and is it healthy? Is your head a safe space?

CHAPTER 9

THE POWER OF WANTING NOTHING FROM PEOPLE WHO HURT YOU

You've been there before. We all have—
where you expect someone to do something,
show appreciation, treat you better, give you
respect, end the verbal abuse, or stop lying—
you know those kinds of people. But for some
reason, you keep giving them concessions or a
pass in the hopes that one day they will be that
kind of person to you—a good person. So you
keep the wrong individuals around even though
they can disrupt your life anytime they want
simply by disappointing you—again and again.
By refusing to adjust your expectations and
create boundaries to protect your well-being
and put yourself first, you allow this to happen.
We place a lot of power in external things, but
boundaries are internal.

You can choose to spend your life wishing
and wanting the people who've hurt you to ask
for your forgiveness. In reality, it's rare when
someone shows up and says, "I'm sorry I hurt
you. Please forgive me." You can want people
to learn from their choices so they don't repeat
them. And most of all, you can want people to
change so they are better for themselves, you,
and others, but therein lies the problem.

Expectations are thoughts, beliefs, ideas, or stories that we create—and if they are not met, then we aren't happy. We tend to have expectations of our partners and assume they should be in tune enough to know certain things about us. They should know when we're sad—and why—when something is bothering us, when anxiety or depression are settling in, and anything else. The problem is that those expectations can easily lead us down a rabbit hole, making us focus on the actions and behaviors of others because we know what we're looking for or expecting. That leads to judgment, mistrust, disappointment, and all those negative thoughts that infiltrate our mindset—and then that process repeats itself.

Expectations are typically unspoken, and lack of communication leads to conflict. You can tell someone to clean the kitchen, but what does that mean to them? What does that mean to you? Cleaning the kitchen may mean loading the dishwasher and turning it on to some people. To you, it may include loading the dishwasher and turning it on, putting things away, sweeping and mopping the floor, cleaning the counters, wiping down the cabinets, and cleaning out the refrigerator. Your idea of something can vastly differ from what your partner, spouse, or children think about the same thing—and if they don't get it right, the only thing it can do is cause some degree of disappointment. Right?

There are a few places where expectations are clarified, such as in the military, when you apply for a job, academic settings, sports, restaurants, and even with therapists. The difference is that those expectations are outlined for people to follow. But when you're driving and let someone over but they don't wave in appreciation, or when you hold the door open for a stranger expecting that they will say thank you, those are personal expectations. When they aren't met, you might get a little road rage or be upset, but that's due to your expectations—not someone else's actions. With expectations, you're giving control and responsibility to the other person hoping they respect you, but we cannot control the behaviors of others. When people don't meet our expectations, we lose trust, but that's not their fault—it's ours.

To sustain a healthier mindset, turn expectations into boundaries and explain them rather

....

**Expectations
are typically
unspoken,
and lack of
communication
leads to
conflict.**

....

than expecting that someone should know what they are and honor them. Boundaries are important to our mental health because they create a healthy structure along with limits that are less restrictive, and they leave room for several outcomes. Expectations are for others, but boundaries are internal and for you to uphold; yet there's a level of accountability that comes with boundaries. That's how I learned to reframe the picture. I don't care if others do something that I don't do, and I don't need to explain myself. They can ask me to change any way they want, but because I've set boundaries for myself, their pushing won't change me. When it comes to my mental health, I've found boundaries to be safer than expectations.

One of the healthiest decisions I've made that has contributed to my well-being is that I learned to want nothing from people who have a pattern of hurting or disappointing me. That's how you jump off that cyclical pattern of behavior, the hamster wheel, that they will keep you on while having no intent to change their path. Stay there, and you are committing to sustaining the same unhealthy mindset. Stop expecting so much of people who are incapable of giving it to you—and that's all there is to it. There are occasions when we set the expectations for someone, and they're just too high. If you use the power of observation, you'll see the pattern that person has with others, and determine whether their behavior is ingrained. The only person you can change is you. It's up to others to change themselves. Sorry, but you don't have that much control over anyone—although some may allow you to think you do.

Save your goals and realistic expectations for yourself and what you aim to accomplish, who you want to become, the way you treat others, your response to adverse situations, and when you walk away, which are all aspects within *your* control. Establishing boundaries for yourself will take the focus off others as well as the disappointments. Boundaries protect us. The Centers for Disease Control and Prevention guidelines for COVID-19 instructed us to have boundaries—wear a mask and maintain a safe physical distance—but with expectations, we can only hope that others will follow the rules. Can you make them do that? No.

....

The only person you can change is you. It's up to others to change themselves.

....

Sometimes people are living with their guilt, pain, or some degree of suffering while others may have none. Either way, it has to be OK because those are events in *their* life. It's not up to you to decide how they should feel or what they should do. If they choose to do anything, that's their responsibility. Being angry because someone doesn't act according to how you think they should can keep in you in a world of pain, depression, and anger. I was there, but not any longer. Again—you will learn that you can't control others, so let it go and work on what you *can* control.

When you are genuinely content with yourself, you will come to realize you don't need family, friends, associates, or anyone to function. I've found that I don't want the approval of people who lack self-awareness. I'm leery of those types of individuals because they can pull me into frustrating conversations that are not beneficial. In my experience, when people are not willing to change negative char-acteristics about themselves because they won't acknowledge them, I can't change them either. That's their growth and development process so they must be open to new perspectives and consider whether they are thinking or acting appropriately. I continually had to defend myself and justify my position to people who lack self-awareness until I decided that it has been counterproductive.

Some people will focus their attention on intention rather than what actually happened. They will tell you that they are sorry you feel the way you do rather than apologize for their actions. Your intentions should never diminish someone else's experiences.

Furthermore, seek understanding and compassion from people who are capable of giving it to you. You already know who those individuals are, so don't take those conversations elsewhere only to get an inattentive response. That, too, can lead to greater frustration.

I've learned not to take serious conversations to individuals who want to one-up my experiences as though it's a competition when it's not. It's about being heard and understood. I've also learned that some people are toxically positive—meaning they will always find a way to justify the negative. These are not people I want anything from because for them it's not about being objective or fair, it's about winning the conversation. They don't allow you to express yourself by making you believe you need to think about a negative situation more positively than you have. Sure, there is a time for that, but know when that is. When you continue to expect these people to change, know that they're not planning on it. Sometimes you have to want nothing from toxic individuals, those who lack self-awareness, empathy, responsibility, or healthy characteristics as a whole. One thing that has helped me become more self-aware is writing in my journal; pay attention to what you write and evaluate your perspective.

Looking inward helped me heal a lot faster and tap into God and myself to look for what I needed from those two sources rather than everyone else. At some point people will disappoint you, and you have to rebound rather than stay in that place of hurt. What God has to offer has been fulfilling, and, more than anything, it has been beneficial. I believe that not wanting or expecting so much from others is what it means to *be* your own safe space. At the end of the day, you know you can always come back home to yourself where you can be protected and OK— if you invest in your well-being.

I used to wonder who would catch me when I fell, and since I've plummeted off that precipice of mental health, now I know. I caught myself by reconnecting to God. I'm not saying I don't need people. But I don't need the people who have hurt and disappointed me because I've learned to have a level of self-reliance and resilience. It makes me bounce back more quickly. Two things that have been constant in my life are God and Achea, and that has given me the confidence of knowing *I've got this*. Take the steps that will help you learn to trust your- self and rely on yourself so you can say with confidence, "I've got this" too. There is power in cultivating your strength.

When it comes to anxiety and depression, I've found that medication and therapy are 80 percent of what's helping with my mental health, but the other 20 percent is what I have to figure out. Sometimes things aren't that complicated— they just need to be said, done, and reinforced.

....

**Not wanting
or expecting
so much from
others is what
it means to
be your own
safe space.**

....

Is there anyone you need to release? Have you perhaps realized that some relationships are unhealthy, one-sided, or not authentic, and it may be best for you to accept that you want nothing from anyone who hurts you?

CHAPTER 10

WHO ARE YOU?

For the longest time I didn't know who
I was because I was trying to be who I was
groomed to be. No one could see what I was
going through because it was an internal battle.
I didn't know how to act or where I fit; I
didn't know who I was for many years, which
caused many more years of damage. One of
the advantages of knowing who you are is that
you will see where you fit, and you can find
your community.

There are several other benefits to knowing
who you are. If you don't know, begin taking
baby steps to help you venture out, try new
things, and discover what you like. It's important
to your mental well-being to know what
makes you happy or laugh or what captures
your interest in a healthy manner. *Who are you?*
Some people invest in ancestry tests simply to
find out their family ancestry, ethnicity, culture,
genetics, and who they are because they don't
feel a part of anything. Ask questions about your
history so you can learn and have an opportunity to choose. If you don't know, you can't
make a choice. That doesn't mean you have to

conform, but it will help you understand more about yourself.

People desperately try to fit in when it isn't necessarily the right fit. And, of course, as a child, I wanted to please my father and the people around me. So when I was in their presence, I'd morph into the person who made them happy. Consequently I began to do that for friends and others until, well, I lost sight of who I was because it was more important for people to be happy and like me or love me. Why wouldn't I? I had no idea it would come at a steep price and create a turbulent journey. Somewhere along the way, after losing focus on being authentic, I lost myself—which was painful.

If you don't know who you are—even career-wise—then what are you working toward? Think of life as a movie. If you don't know your role, character, or motives, you don't know how to act. You need to know who you are to behave accordingly. This can be applied to anyone. Consider a basketball or football player. If they don't know their position, then they don't know what they're supposed to be

It's important to your mental well-being to know what makes you happy or laugh or what captures your interest in a healthy manner.

doing. They may end up trying to take on roles that don't contribute to a functional system.

If you think about it, we all have roles that come with a definition. A parent, point guard, computer analyst, actor, a person in the military, teacher—all these roles require us to act accordingly. When we don't know who we are we act in ways that don't match, meaning we are not congruent with ourselves, and that can cause additional stress. Sometimes you may feel like a character without any depth, but you've got to work to find yourself.

One of the questions to ask yourself is whether you've ever thought about who you are. If you don't like yourself, it's likely that you've put a lot of thought into it, and something needs to change. I'm not talking about your name and where you're from, but ask yourself: *What is my true identity?* If I asked you to define yourself, what would you say? What characteristics make up *you?* It's essential to have an understanding of yourself. Many people say they've never really given it much thought or confess that they don't know who they are. *Do you?* Your profession or vocation is not who you are but rather what you do. Yet it can tell you what you value—work ethic, money, education, interests, beliefs, character traits, integrity, relationships, or something else. Are you honest? Compassionate? Trustworthy? Spiritual? Loving? Happy? A realist or dreamer? While you may be someone who suffers from anxiety, depression, or some aspect of mental illness, that's not who you are.

Your interests can tell you about your competitive nature, your drive, and your character. I am highly competitive with myself and enjoy activities when me, myself, and I are the competition. I love playing tennis, riding a bike, and doing Pilates. I am self-motivated and resourceful. I'm OK without knowing all the answers, but I will work to find them. I am creative and I love to cook, decorate, and create spaces that make one feel safe. I love to travel, experience new cultures, and appreciate the differences in people—that's a piece of who I am.

Remove the labels that others may have given you and let people begin to see you for who you really are. It can take time, self-discovery, exploration, and the willingness to truly acknowledge who you are not. For some, the issue with recognizing who you are is knowing who you are not. One of the things that happened to me in my self-discovery phase was stripping off labels and discovering who I wasn't, but I didn't have any new labels to replace them. I was in the land of *I don't know,* but it opened the door to discover what fits and works for me and what doesn't.

When you take a look at the things you discard, you'll realize they weren't reflective of you. People are afraid of that *I don't know* period when they're in limbo someplace in their journey. Like being in the cave, you aren't afraid when you can see the light, but you reach fear quickly when you're in the darkness and feel as though you're wading in the unknown.

I asked who you are because *you* need to know—anxiety and depression can be triggered when you don't. Often people will relate a problem, issue, or some negative aspect of something that happened with who they are. Typically, that's because a label has been given to them, which can become a part of their identity. I was labeled as a singer, church girl, serious, virtuous, prim and proper, obedient, a good Christian girl, prissy, superhuman, and unbreakable, but none of that was who I was or who I am today. Those were the labels given to me by my parents, family, friends, and others. I wanted to play soccer because I'm competitive with myself and athletic. As a teenager I didn't drink or do drugs, but I was bored and boy crazy. I was nearly the opposite of all labels given to me, and no one knew me well enough to know that.

For the most part, people have always focused on who I am not. I guess that's easier for some people. Not everyone considers me to be "normal" because I was diagnosed with generalized anxiety disorder, major depressive disorder, and body dysmorphia. While that's a mouthful, that's not who I am. If you have a mental health challenge, that's not who you are either. People with cancer have cancer; they are not cancer. People with COVID-19 have COVID-19; they are not COVID-19. That's why most people don't know me. I am not a mental illness, and I wasn't born with one. I suffer from the diagnosis I've been given, which developed in the environment I grew up in—*home*.

If you ask me who I am, I will tell you. I am the most caring, empathetic, passionate, justice-driven human being that I know. I wish I had a friend like me. But maybe my expectations have been too high. People *aren't* me. They aren't you. And again, as hard of a lesson as that has been, that's OK, too, because whether we keep people in our lives who aren't good people is our choice. We give the wrong people access and authority over our lives when we accept who they are and still let them in.

I've started building the foundation of becoming safer for myself and being my own best friend instead of taking what I can get. That's settling. Taking these steps makes me feel good and proud in a humble way because I couldn't say that before. I didn't say anything. Therefore, I wasn't putting my well-being first, as if doing so was selfish. But it's not. If I'm not OK, I can't take care of the people I love or anyone else, as I've demonstrated. I went off that precipice because I wasn't taking adequate care of myself. If I had been, that *never* would have occurred. Emotionally, mentally, and physically, it's possible to be pushed beyond what you can

handle, and you don't want to find that out
by default. Now that I know how my mental
health and well-being are now, and moving
forward, this is one of the ways I am protecting
my future.

When it comes to relationships, personal
or professional, when I'm in, I'm all in. If I'm
out, I'm out. Even though I knew I was a damn
good human being, a good friend, mother, and
amazing wife, the way people treated me caused
me to doubt myself. Not trusting yourself leads
to not trusting others. Your relationship with
yourself crafts the other relationships in your
life—when it's critical.

I decided to become a mental health advo-
cate because of my struggles, so I dove in,
studied, and learned as much as I could on the
topic. If a psychiatrist was going to diagnose me
with something, I wanted to know everything I
could on the subject to understand it and better
understand me before I accepted the diagnosis.
I am a lifetime student and I love learning. It
doesn't matter if I'm learning by listening, in
conversations, or by reading a book; I crave
knowledge and learning about people's lives.

205

I am curious by nature and I'm not afraid to ask questions. I want people to be honest and comfortable doing the same with me.

If you want to know who you are, invest in understanding yourself, how your body works or doesn't, the way medications affect you, natural ways to diffuse stressful situations and release stress, what makes you happy, whom you can trust, and where your safe space is—ensuring you have one. Ask questions and pay attention.

Most of what I know about people I didn't learn because of what they told me; it came through observation. Minor observations can reveal who has invested in knowing who you are. It's the little things that are significant indicators of whether people care and hear me. If they don't, I can't change that, but at least I am aware and don't expect anything.

If someone purchases a gift or an ornament when they travel and brings one back for me, that's an individual who has heard me. They're aware I collect ornaments from everywhere we travel. You can't go wrong buying me a cool coffee mug with an empowering message or a

....

**If you want
to know who
you are,
invest in
understanding
yourself.**

....

little souvenir from someplace I've never been.
And I love things that bring comfort. I love
when I go out with my husband or friends, and
they're aware that I love doing the things they've
planned because they know who I am. If you
know me, you know these details about me.

Pay attention to the things people take
the initiative to do for you or what they know
about you. If they don't know, attempt to help
them learn about your authentic self. Perhaps
you haven't shown them. If they are not invested
in knowing you—the real you—consider what
that relationship is about. I've decided to focus
on those who honor the person I am, which is
reciprocated. However, I became burned out
from those taking my energy without replacing
it with more good energy. I had to step away
and stop investing in so many others when I
needed to take better care of myself.

I went to lunch with one of my friends, and
as soon as the server brought my iced tea and
placed it in front of me, my friend smiled and
said, "You might want to bring her a whole plate
of lemons and more ice, please." It felt good to
notice that she had made those observations

about me. Outside of her, there has been no one else who knows that little detail about me. The point is that you want people to pay attention to you so they can see you—*you*! And it matters because I noticed. People don't know who you are if they overlook the bare basics, such as those little standards or routine behaviors. As for the people who notice, those are the ones who typically care. I've always found it easy to care about people, but I had to create a healthier network of people who genuinely care about me too. And I've found that to be happy and healthy, change is good.

I learned that I have to tackle one thing at a time. When you start to love yourself you will discard some of the core beliefs that have been instilled in you or that you've instilled in yourself because you will find that a negative mindset has been working against you all along. I've thought about the things I've been told and realized they weren't true. I found that I want people to see me without labels, adverse history, or anything else.

CHAPTER 11

THE CAUSES OF GRIEF

Grief and loss encompass more than the death of someone. It's about losing yourself as a result of trauma. It's a change in how you see yourself with other people. Sometimes people need a moment to grieve that things are no longer the same. We may come to realize that our bodies aren't able to do something the same as before and we don't get a chance to grieve that our bodies are changing. Consider an athlete who sustains a career-ending injury, or someone who has lost mobility, had an accident or a health crisis, struggled with obesity, or changed as people age naturally. All of these can be losses to people. Sports, being active, working, traveling—these are things people enjoy. And when they can no longer do them, it can cause them to go through the process of grieving.

You can't fix something that's gone, but you can work to process it and celebrate the time you had. One of the ways to accept the loss is to spend time acknowledging it. Ask yourself what that thing or person provided. If it is solitude, perhaps you can look for something else that will provide solitude. If you've lost a friendship with someone you could confide in or laugh

....

Sometimes people need a moment to grieve that things are no longer the same.

....

with, it may take time to develop a new friendship, but being open to that happening can help.

One of the most complex parts of therapy was grieving the loss of what I wanted and needed and letting them go. For me, grieving the loss of someone living is a hell of a lot worse than some would imagine. A part of my depression has been lamenting and grieving over the childhood I lost, parents I needed, and the loss of a father. Depression is rumination over the past and anxiety is rumination over the future, and they often coincide. I grieved the past and what I didn't have, although my relationship with my father wasn't healthy.

Why? I grieved the concept of what my father was supposed to be and that I didn't have the potential of repairing or creating a healthy relationship with him. It was the loss of an opportunity and what my father represented. I went through life grieving potential or the lack thereof—a loss of identity, a parent, a loss of anything. At times I felt isolated and alone. What happened to me during COVID-19 happened because I was still grieving those losses. I wasn't taking care of myself or focused on anything I should have been, and it was disastrous.

I asked Mom what I was like as a child. She told me I was very shy and grew out of it a little. I'm not socially awkward when I know you, but as a rule, I'm quiet. I don't give that openness to everybody. Mom said I was the kind of kid who hid behind her leg when someone approached her; I didn't like attention on myself. But the truth is that I grieved not being more outgoing like my father. I asked Mom if I was a happy child, and she said, "Yes, when you were with me." Then Mom added, "If you weren't going somewhere, you were locked up in your room." I replied, "You thought I was happy? Man, I remember things differently."

And that, too, became a part of my grieving—grieving the lack of awareness. I can't get others to open that Pandora's box and reveal the truth, but I have to do it. There will be those moments when difficult conversations happen with a family member, friend, or therapist, but when you leave that person, that's when the work is tested, and you have to process the grief, come to terms with it, and sit in the loss.

There will be those
moments when difficult
conversations happen
with a family member,
friend, or therapist,
but when you leave
that person, that's
when the work is
tested, and you have
to process the grief,
come to terms with it,
and sit in the loss.

I've been to enough therapy to know when that is, and I am better equipped to discern what to do with those feelings. When you learn how to process grief and go through loss, I can't say it gets easier, but you become more proficient. I am learning to grieve and work with the best that I've got. Some people may be unaware because they prefer not to address or accept their situation and be held accountable for their role. I am learning to be OK with that because I can't control them.

Is there something you've been grieving? How are you managing? Is it something you should speak to a professional therapist about to learn coping skills?

CHAPTER 12

THE BATTLE OF THE MINDS

When I think back over my life through the lens I had while battling anxiety and depression, those thoughts, the history swirling around in my mind, the things I witnessed and experienced, and the "what-ifs" become a dangerous combination. None of my siblings will look at our history and see an identical story or share the same perspective. People adapt to and learn different things from most situations. We're on the same planet, but some people see the sun rising while others see it setting. We may have been in the same classroom with other students and some may embrace the teacher's style of teaching while others struggle. Two siblings can grow up in the same household and turn out very different.

One may say, "Let me take these experiences and use them as fuel to get out of this environment, get a scholarship and get into the best school so that I can be the best. I'm going to prove who I can be." That individual chooses to work hard to get out of a difficult or negative situation. The other sibling may have a different perspective of their experiences; the internal conversation is pessimistic, and the self-talk is harmful. They think, *I can't think about anything but this, and it's holding me back. I can't move past this. This is my life, this is my world, and I'm stuck.* Those are maladaptive and negative thoughts that impede growth. And if you truly believe that you're stuck, you're not growing, you don't have any potential, and those experiences are what's holding you back—then why would you grow? How can you possibly grow if you're telling yourself all these negative things?

Among other factors, when you're holding yourself back, there is some responsibility that has to come with that. You can regain a lot of control when you recognize that you play a part in your growth. If you believe these external factors are the cause of who and what you are, then you lose control and eventually live your life as if it is out of control—you've relinquished it to history, to others, and to negative experiences.

Your mindset plays such a huge part in your growth because it all depends on how you look at things. We've seen child stars in the media. Some have breakdowns, and while we can't speak to all of their experiences, they come out

....

**You can
regain a lot
of control
when you
recognize
that you play
a part in
your growth.**

....

with tremendous issues. Then there are others who have unblemished reputations and appear happy, yet we can't speak to all of their experiences either. Some people can't take the pressure and crumble, while others can take it and rise. They strive to be their best. But, again, the public has expectations of these individuals. We expect that since they are doing great things, they should have a great life. Those are our expectations. Placing expectations on others is just as bad as having them put on us.

People say a lot of things to themselves internally. You probably wouldn't say the things to other people or friends that you say to yourself—but you definitely give that negative self-talk to yourself, and you are likely to believe it. Still, you wouldn't stand on a stage in front of an audience and say negative things about yourself because they're private, but you would say them to yourself. It's similar to how you act in your own space; you might walk around half-dressed and hair undone, but you wouldn't go outside that way.

These types of thoughts may come at night because you have a moment of privacy, and that's when they tend to surface. But don't keep them in your head. Instead, grab a pen and paper and write them down. Write everything that you say to yourself—and then read them. What did you say? "I hate the way I look." "I suck." "I'm unsuccessful." "I'm fat." "I won't get that raise." You're convincing yourself of that negative self-talk. Before you know it, you've done such a great job you'll wake up and take those damaging, negative thoughts with you day after day. You're going to believe it. And the expectations we have of ourselves are not isolated to people with anxiety, depression, or mental illness. We compare ourselves to others or the standards set by society, and when we think we're not meeting those standards, this is the conversation we end up having. This has to change.

The way to avoid negative self-talk is to put yourself on trial and argue against what you are trying to convince yourself of. If you can say, "Yes, I make a ton of mistakes," that's a whole different thing. Perhaps you have some character traits to work on. But when you say, "I'm stupid," "I make mistakes all the time," "No one loves me," "Everyone hates me," look

at the other side of that argument. You may
be in college, have graduated, are successful in
your career or fulfilled, and have loyal family or
friends even if it's one or two individuals. You
may be kind, compassionate, and have children
who love and appreciate you and a partner
whom you love and care about. Whatever is
on your list—and you have a good one—some
qualities contradict the conflicting thoughts
peeling away your self-esteem through that self-
talk you're entertaining inside your head.

People told me that I wasn't a people person
or friendly, that I was closed off, a snob, lazy,
overly sensitive, dramatic, and spoiled. I am a
people person when I want to be. When I know
you, I'm one of the friendliest people. However,
if you're throwing off a vibe that reveals I can't
trust you—yes, I'm closed off. I don't do that
out of maliciousness; it's done out of self-protec-
tion. I won't close you off if I don't feel I need
to protect myself. I'm one of the most down-to-
earth people you will ever meet. I don't brag or
boast. I'm not overly confident; I'm grounded.
Lazy—hell, no! I am overly sensitive; I am an
empath. I can feel, and that's one of the best

The way to
avoid negative
self-talk is to
put yourself on
trial and argue
against what
you are trying
to convince
yourself of.

qualities about me as a human being. I'm not
a pessimist or an optimist—I am a realist. Am I
dramatic? I think toxically positive people are
the ones who accuse me of being dramatic. They
don't want to accept the reality that things are
what they are. As far as being spoiled? OK, I am
spoiled and love it. I have enough self-confi-
dence to believe I deserve the wonderful things
I get and not feel guilty about it. In essence, my
battle of the mind caused me to talk myself into
feeling guilty, unworthy, bad, or sad or to accept
things. Either way, going through that meant I
had to better understand who I was.

You get what you give in life, and I provide
a lot of positive energy and good; whatever
good comes back to me—I deserve it. We allow
society to make us think that being spoiled
and successful are negative when they're not.
Rather than accept the things people say about
you, challenge them as you would in a debate.
Be fair and look at it from the outside. Where
is the evidence that it is true and where is
the evidence that it is false? Then change that
false statement. You are human, and sometimes
you will make poor decisions just like other

human beings do; you just may not see their poor decisions.

Since I'd mastered the art of negative self-talk, I had to learn how to challenge those thoughts and ideas and win the internal battles to refrain from convincing myself of terrible outcomes. I was bombarded by fear, a lack of confidence, and inadequacy—and quick to believe that "I wasn't" or "I couldn't." Therefore, internally, I had no peace, and of course my mind wasn't a safe space. The internal turmoil from intrusive thoughts inside my head was unbearable. I'd constantly ruminate, yet no one could see this going on. No one knew how damaging that self-talk was to me and how I had to fight to present a strong, confident persona, which wasn't me. Doing so produced unnecessary stress.

Sometimes people twist your mind so you believe negative things about yourself, and you become enslaved to the thoughts others have about you that then become your own. Every negative idea I had about myself came from someone else. I thought being spoiled, overly sensitive, and all those other things were negatives, and I adapted them until I discovered I loved those traits about myself and no longer battle them in my mind. I saw myself the way other people saw me until I realized I wasn't any of those negative things that were said about me. Sometimes we tend to take what happens to us and make it a reason to adopt a victim mentality. We take abuse and victimization and make it our own. That doesn't have to be the case when we fight the battle and address our self-talk.

Do you have beliefs or thoughts about yourself that you battle in your mind? Do you have a different perspective than others in your household? How can you turn your thoughts into power?